What next for Labour?

Ideas for a new generation

What next for Labour?

Ideas for a new generation

Edited by: Tom Scholes-Fogg and Hisham Hamid

Queensferry PUBLISHERS

Typeset by Elaine Sharples
Printed by PODW in Great Britain.

Queensferry Publishing Limited
145 – 157
St John Street
London
EC1V 4PW
www.queensferrypublishing.co.uk

ISBN: 978-1-908570-00-0

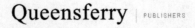

Acknowledgements

We would like to sincerely thank those who contributed to this book for their cooperation and hard work. We would like to thank in particular Baroness Mary Goudie for her help and advice when putting this together. We hope this book can fulfil its aim in bringing together different ideas and contribute to the debate on the future of the Labour Party.

Contents

Introduction

Tom Scholes-Fogg
and Hisham Hamid

We embarked on this project with the aim of bringing together ideas from a diverse range of people within the Labour Party and presenting their thoughts in one place, on what they think the future is for Labour. For the first time in nearly a decade and a half the Labour Party is in opposition and as a result is able to have an open and honest debate. A debate about what the future of the party is ideologically – about who the Party represents, and most importantly – what the Labour Party stands for.

Our humble attempt of contributing to this discussion is by no means comprehensive, but it's a welcome start. Our intention was to try and extend the discourse about Labour's future from beyond the highest echelons of the Party. The concept of collating ideas from those on the left and right of the party including essays from Members of Parliament, Peers of the realm, former ministers in government, current shadow ministers and grass roots activists, is a novel way of presenting this debate in an accessible way, which we hope will invite both members and those outside of the Party to engage in the process of Labour's revival. We chose not to present any specific narrative – but decided to leave the debate open-ended for readers to consider.

Unlike conventional edited collections, for this book we opted for more contributors and asked them to consolidate their thoughts into less than three thousand words. We have been fortunate in securing these contributors; the quality and depth of insight explored in their pieces is remarkable.

Ed Miliband has been the leader of the Labour Party for a year; critics say he has yet to show real leadership and lay out his vision for where he wants to take the Labour Party. Supporters of Miliband say he is making progress slowly but surely. What is clear is that he faces many challenges, such as demonstrating Labour has learnt lessons from the past and that his shadow cabinet are a credible government in waiting. The Labour leader has a short amount of time to rebuild support among huge swathes of the electorate, and convince them that the Labour Party is the best alternative to the Conservative led Coalition.

After an historic thirteen years in government, the Labour Party has achieved a great deal. Criticism and mistakes aside – it would be hard to argue that Britain is not a better place for it. Labour has a record it can be proud of – crime down by a third, more police on the streets, the New Deal, the minimum wage, civil partnerships, devolution, peace in Northern Ireland, investment in education and the NHS, Sure Start, Child Tax Credits and the Winter Fuel Allowance. The list of Labour achievements goes on.

However, Labour's time in government was overshadowed by many mistakes, some of which were responsible for alienating many disenfranchised voters. The expectations of what a Labour government could achieve, after an historic landslide victory in 1997 faded during its time in office. The war in Iraq and the war on terror that followed was a significant error of judgement – coupled with Tony Blair's alignment with a neo-conservative US president. The erosion of civil liberties – proposing the introduction of ID cards, the use of stop and search powers – which were often employed for entirely the wrong reasons, and the proposed 90 days to hold a suspect without charge. All of which were an attack on individual freedom and liberty, as a result of a knee jerk reaction to the perceived threat of terrorism. The fact of the matter is that the Labour Party got it wrong on these issues, and any attempt to reintroduce them as policies would be met with great hostility.

Widespread criticism has been levelled against Labour's immigration policy, which has led to a loss of support among a section of Labour's core support. The problem has been Labour's failure in addressing issues important to the white working classes – such as housing, welfare and jobs. Neglecting to communicate clearly with such a crucial part of Labour's electoral demographic has led to a vacuum being created, which is now being filled by extremist right-wing parties, such as the British National Party – who have capitalised on these issues, and have used them as an opportunity to further their own xenophobic ideological narrative, and create racial tensions within our communities. Labour has also failed to communicate the importance of the contribution migrants have made to Britain – specifically to the British economy. Immigration is an important factor in explaining why Labour lost so many DE voters between 1997 and 2010. Indeed, in Lord Whitty's contribution, he defines Labour's core vote as consisting of "three main elements: traditional white working class, liberal professionals, and ethnic minorities".

To understand the challenges that currently face the Labour party, it is crucial to acknowledge the profound contribution made by the New Labour project and its proponents. When Mrs Thatcher was asked what her greatest political achievement was, she responded "New Labour", which is certainly true. New Labour was a response to the seismic change in the British political landscape after eighteen years of Conservative government. What the 'modernisers' in the party understood, was that Labour needed to incorporate this change, by accepting the neo-liberal economic reforms of the Conservatives – embracing and encouraging the role of the market – promising a commitment to low taxation, accepting trade union reforms and adopting a hard line on crime, justice and defence.

Pragmatism has taken on a new meaning in British politics, and to some within the Labour Party it has its negative connotations – to many it denotes abandoning ideals and principles for the sake of power. But Labour has historically been at its best when it is at its most pragmatic – from the establishment of the welfare state and the NHS to the liberal reforms of the 1960s to even giving the Bank of England independence.

New Labour was political pragmatism at its best. Its centrist approach is why Blair and the New Labour project was left wholly unopposed for so long. If there is one lesson worth learning from the Conservative Party, it is the importance of pragmatism – the twentieth century dominated by a Conservative hegemony is proof of this. The most important aspect of New Labour worth retaining is the notion that Labour is a party of government – not opposition. Adopting a non-dogmatic approach, being flexible with political realities and forming policy respectively, are the way into government – real change can only be achieved while in power. This is why a focus on winning elections is critically important for the Labour Party to move forward.

Labour's Complacency

One year into Ed Miliband's leadership the party has failed to make any substantial progress in developing distinct policies – which is beginning to take its toll. The narrative on the economy is particularly an area where the Labour party has failed to make its mark. There is a sense of complacency from some within the party, who appear to think that the Coalition Government will simply hang itself with their deeply unpopular cuts agenda.

There exists a perception that the Coalition will redress the

4

deficit through draconian cuts – and at next election Labour will be swept into power on the promise of re-investment in public services and the economy. With this strategy there is a risk Labour will be punished at the ballot box for having created a situation which allowed the government cuts to take place. Were the Labour Party to have won the 2010 General Election – would a Labour government have been prepared to deal with the enormous backlash from having to enforce similarly deep cuts to public spending in order to balance the books?

The Coalition Government is scathingly critical of Labour's economic record and places blame at the door of the last government for Britain's structural deficit. One of the most prominent critiques is the fact that the Labour Government ran a large budget deficit in the mid-part of the last decade when the economy was booming – as opposed to running a surplus. But the rationale is quite understandable; it was not sheer mindless profligacy as Brown's intent was to redress the chronic under-investment in public services and infrastructure left by successive Conservative governments. It is worth noting that David Cameron and his party pledged to match Labour's spending plans, while also calling for *less* financial regulation when in opposition, whereas the Liberal Democrats were advocating an *increase* in public spending. This suggests that, either the opposition parties now in government were equally incompetent in understanding the ramifications of Britain's large structural deficit and high levels of public spending, or were just blatantly opportunistic in their promises – either way; it makes their assessment of Labour's economic record look superficial.

A legitimate criticism levelled against Labour's economic record, was the attitude that if money were thrown at public services then standards would improve de facto. This led to huge inefficiency in how public money was spent, with little accountability and poor consideration about its effectiveness. Costly capital projects under Private Finance Initiatives, and the establishment of Quango after Quango are prime examples of this. So much more could have been achieved with less, if public money was targeted more effectively. This in turn, would have meant a lower or even non-existent structural deficit while the economy was experiencing accelerated growth. The underlying weakness of debt in the British economy was exposed dramatically when the structural deficit reached unsustainable levels due to the Government's colossal cash injection into the economy in response to the economic crisis of 2008–09.

Unfortunately New Labour was convinced by the city's apparent invincibility, and believed there would be continued unparalleled economic growth. The fact of the matter is, Labour failed miserably on market regulation, even with the introduction of the Financial Services Authority (FSA). The problem lay in the fact that, after years of expounding the credo of 'no more boom and bust', Labour was convinced it had actually achieved this. Congratulatory praises and over-reliance on the city, led to a perception of infallibility which Labour fell for. It overlooked the fact that Labour's role historically has been to temper and redress the excesses of turbo-capitalism – but it totally failed – New Labour worshipped the markets.

The Contributors
The contributors to this book tackle a whole host of issues and include figures from the party's past and present, including former Labour General Secretary, Lord Larry Whitty, who, in his piece, analyses Labour's electoral support and explores the philosophy of social democracy. Lecturer of Sociology at Kingston University, Dr Rupa Huq, considers in-depth the importance of suburban support in Labour's path back to power. Former First Sea Lord, Admiral Lord Alan West, looks at Britain's defence capabilities in light of reductions in public spending. Tracy J Cheetham outlines the importance of embracing social media as an excellent means of mobilizing

support at grass roots level, and utilising its huge potential as a campaigning tool. Bill Esterson MP calls upon the party to rediscover its roots and former Conservative and Labour MP, Lord Peter Temple-Morris, suggests the Labour Party considers changing its name as part of the renewal process.

Former Schools minister, Lord Jim Knight, looks back at Labour's achievements in education and asks how we can gear the system to truly enable social mobility. Former NUS president, Aaron Porter, and Former Labour MP, Nick Palmer, explore options for an equitable approach to funding higher education. Axel Landin highlights the need for Labour to reaffirm its status as the party of the younger generation.

On the economy, Councillor for Elton, James Frith, explains the ever-growing importance of encouraging and supporting small businesses as the engines of economic growth, whereas Matt Pitt puts forward the case for a British Investment bank. On the NHS, President of the Royal Society for Public Health, Lord Phillip Hunt, looks back at one of Labour's greatest achievements in government, transforming the NHS, and outlines how Labour should tackle the Coalition's proposed NHS reorganisation. Women, Equality and Poverty campaigner Baroness Mary Goudie stresses the importance of Britain's role in supporting international aid and development – even through difficult economic circumstances. Labour's future for the green agenda is tackled by Kieran Roberts and Shadow Minister for Environment, Food and Rural Affairs, William Bain MP, explains the growing role of green industries in the British economy and how we must harness them.

Looking Ahead

The new landscape in British politics created after the 2010 general election has dramatically altered the role of the Labour Party. Looking forward, the party must develop and establish an ideological narrative, principles and a set of polices in a new political climate, which reflects who the Labour Party represents, and sets out its vision for Britain.

For Labour to win the next election, it has to reach out to disenfranchised voters and listen to their concerns. Ed Miliband was right to say that the Labour Party was too comfortable in government and as a result, neglected those who mattered most. The importance of reaching out and trying to attract a broad coalition of support in this revival process is crucial.

Not enough effort has been made by the Labour Party to engage with the public, disenfranchised voters, and former party supporters. Failure to reach out will perpetuate the sense of disconnect between many former Labour supporters that feel the party no longer represents them, and its policies no longer address their needs. In general, this apparent disdain towards the political class is only worsened by the arrogance of politicians in the way they interact with voters. If they aren't being evasive, disingenuous or just patronising, they are often talking amongst themselves. Dialogue very rarely extends beyond party cliques and discussions are often unconstructive, as they hardly ever stray from party political point-scoring. If the Labour Party is to be honest it can hardly claim that it is setting the agenda on this issue. As Ann Black explains in her piece, "there are more than 20 shadow cabinet review groups whose membership is hidden even from the National Executive Committee".

Unfortunately, there is a crisis of political engagement with mainstream politics that exists within large parts of British Society – the most important of which includes an entire generation of young people. This crisis is an issue that must be addressed directly by the Labour Party. What is obvious, is choosing not to participate in the political process creates an unfortunate cycle of those not voting being unable to have a say. The relevance of policies made by political parties is shaped around people who choose to vote. Parties tend to focus on attracting support and creating policies around those who engage in the political process – who generally tend to be middle-class, affluent, educated, middle-aged and white.

All mainstream political parties are responsible for failing to make young people feel like stakeholders in the political process, and more widely in society, as we have seen with the recent riots. An effective way for Labour to tackle this issue is to create a campaign to introduce more comprehensive political education as part of the National Curriculum. This already exists to a very small degree at secondary level, through Citizenship Studies. Developing an objective yet rigorous syllabus on the fundamentals of the British political system would bring untold benefit, to not only young people themselves – but for democracy and society as a whole. What many Social Science teachers will tell you is the degree of positive participation that students engage in when issues which are relevant to them and their daily lives, are the subject of discussion. Labour should be at the forefront of this campaign if it is to realistically build support and inspire a new generation of politically aware and active young people.

So much of this disconnect can be attributed to simply being unaware of how the political process works – who the political parties are and what they stand for – and most importantly, what it means to them. Galvanising support is a relatively easy task once young people begin to appreciate the huge number of political issues that affect them. Young people often fail to see the link between the issues they care about and its inextricable link to mainstream politics and government policy. The perception of politicians as remote, alien figures that speak of things they do not understand – let alone care about, needs to be broken. Young people often express their disinterest in politics and political issues – but when asked how they feel about NHS reforms or EMA being abolished, or tuition fees trebling, the economy and job prospects for the future – they express their passion – *they engage in the debate.* What must be communicated is that to have any real impact on what is happening around them, they must participate in the mainstream political process, which ultimately means voting.

An emphasis on more comprehensive political education should be coupled with the campaign for lowering the voting age to 16. This would be a great move in empowering young people to participate in the political process. This would allow so many, who often do not get the chance to vote until their twenties, the added window of an extra two years to have their say. The message needs to be made clear – voting is an empowering aspect of being a part of society. It is such a shame that so many young people fail to see the importance of this crucial part of active citizenship. Getting young people to engage in the political process should a central part of Labour's strategy to rebuild support. In his piece, Axel Landin quite rightly suggests, "Young people have the potential to be the driving force behind Labour's return to power". Labour needs to concentrate a huge amount of its efforts in engaging with younger people in an easily accessible and relevant discourse – as the Labour Party is the natural recipient of the support from this key, yet so neglected demographic.

The Challenge

There is a clamour for the mantle of 'the progressive party' in British politics – the reality is that Labour is the only legitimate choice – providing that the party reforms. Our view is clear – the Labour Party is the only real alternative to the ideological agenda of the Tories and the Orange Book Liberals. However, simply opposing the cuts will not be enough to gain support and secure votes – it did not work during the 1980s nor will it work now. Failing to develop a credible economic plan will allow the Tories to erode the Labour Party's record on economic competence – which will ultimately cost Labour the next general election if it is not addressed robustly.

Labour has had to work hard during its last period in opposition and throughout its time in government to develop its reputation for economic competence – it risks damaging this by not being more vigorous in its explanation for decisions made in government and, more importantly, providing a credible alternative to the Coalition plan on deficit reduction. The mantra of the coalition of 'we are having to clean up the mess left by the last government', if said enough times, and for long enough, is more effective than one might think. It is clear that the Coalition will fight the next election on its economic record and present the argument that it made the tough decisions on the economy and tackled the deficit. For Labour, there is the imminent danger that failure to develop a coherent economic strategy, which is both comprehensive and realistic, and which robustly addresses Britain's vast structural deficit, could damage their economic credibility for a generation.

Ed Miliband doesn't exactly need a Clause IV moment, but he does need to make his mark – and fast. He has yet to lay out his vision for the Labour party. What is clear is that any development should be gradual – the Labour leader is not reinventing the wheel. Labour needs to focus on being radical in government – not in opposition. That is where New Labour fell short – it pandered to the right too often, alienating and taking for granted its core support, and ultimately failed to live up to its promise. It is clear that Labour's legacy has shifted the centre ground of British politics leftwards – the modern 'compassionate' Conservative Party is testament to that fact.

The task for Labour is threefold – the party has to forensically examine its time in government and identify the failures of the Blair and Brown era, understand and accept what Labour got wrong, as well as what made the party successful – and clearly communicate the lessons learnt to the electorate. Labour must exercise realism in its approach to policy – most importantly on the economy, as the Coalition's argument on deficit reduction is dominating the economic narrative. Its strategy of shifting blame onto the last government is effective and is proving successful in obscuring Labour's response. Most importantly, Labour must set the agenda – planning for the future through investment and a fresh approach to the economy with dynamic new ideas.

Labour's path back to power need not be long; rebuilding support is a collective endeavour that many will choose to embrace if Ed Miliband and the Labour Party are honest, profound and forthright in how they communicate with the people. Consigning the party back to the opposition benches gives an unparalleled opportunity to rebuild the party, and to once again become the party of government. We have entered a new period in British politics, which requires a renewed response from a reformed Labour Party. These really are ideas for a new generation, and it is not so much a blank sheet of paper, more of a turning of the page.

Labour's Future

Ann Black

In and Out of Power:
A View from the Grass Roots

Ann Black is secretary of the Oxford East Labour Party and a member of UNISON. She has served as a constituency representative on Labour's National Policy Forum since 1997 and on the National Executive Committee from 2000.

For far too long Labour claimed to have abolished not only the economic cycle of boom-and-bust, but the political cycle as well. Tony Blair spoke often of Labour as the natural party of government for the 21st century. Yet now the wind has changed, and thirteen full years could vanish without trace. How can Labour avoid another lengthy spell in opposition and return to productive power?

The message from history is that governments will not lose elections unless there is a credible alternative: an opposition party will not simply float into Downing Street on a tide of dissatisfaction with the incumbents. This analysis looks at the requirements for winning again, then at Tony Blair's New Labour, which brought electoral success but also sowed the seeds for its own downfall, and finally at what Labour needs now in this new decade.

First, a party should react fast and intelligently to defeat. Labour's 1979 loss followed financial troubles, the IMF bail-out and the winter of discontent, summed up in the Saatchi slogan "Labour isn't working". This narrative ran unchallenged for so long that few now recall anything positive from the Wilson/Callaghan era. The 1983 manifesto simply told the voters again that they, not the party, were wrong. With the SDP breakaway reinforcing perceptions of left-wing extremism, Old Labour was fatally damaged and only wholesale rebranding could rebuild credibility.

The Tories lost in 1997 after Britain's eviction from the exchange rate mechanism, rampant in-fighting over Europe, and cash-for-questions. They were seen as incompetent, divided and unsympathetic: as Theresa May's "nasty party". It took a fuzzy new logo and a fresh leader with family experience of the NHS and warm words on poverty and the environment to change their image and restore electoral appeal.

In 2010 the economy was again the central issue, and as in 1979 an unelected prime minister hesitated over calling an early election with fatal consequences. Under Gordon Brown Labour failed to gain credit for saving the banking system, or for Sure Start, the minimum wage, the right to roam, civil partnerships, new schools, falling hospital waiting times, inroads into child and pensioner poverty, and peace in Northern Ireland. From the first day onwards coalition ministers have repeated the mantra that Labour left the country in a mess and savage cuts are the only remedy. Labour have not rebutted Tory myths, nor celebrated many proud achievements. We can either defend our record or abandon it, and it may already be too late to choose.

Second, an opposition must inspire activists and voters with an alternative vision. No-one expects a line-by-line manifesto, and John Smith's 1992 shadow budget showed the folly of giving hostages to fortune, but Labour badly wants headline pledges, dividing lines and directions of travel. Ed Miliband's sheet of paper cannot stay blank when there are elections every year. It is not enough to jeer at the coalition for its numerous U-turns. When change is for the worse they should be harried, but when it is for the better they should be congratulated for coming round to our position. And we should quit trying to out-tough the coalition on immigration, asylum, prisons, disability benefits and welfare in general. It goes against Labour's deepest values and it will still never convince those who get their facts from the Express and the Mail.

Third, the leader must appear as a potential prime minister, and the shadow cabinet as a government in waiting. After 1997 the Tories chose William Hague, then Iain Duncan Smith, then Michael Howard, and only hit the jackpot with David Cameron. After 1979 Labour elected Michael Foot, then Neil Kinnock. John Smith was never put to the test, but Tony Blair's youth and energy helped to sweep Labour into Downing Street. The party also boasted a heavyweight front bench: Gordon Brown, Robin Cook, Clare Short, Mo Mowlam, David Blunkett, Margaret Beckett and John Prescott. The jury is still out on Ed Miliband, but few would recognise most of today's shadow cabinet.

Fourth, a party requires money to campaign, and this is more forthcoming when in government for obvious if unsavoury reasons. In opposition the Tories rely on a handful of very rich donors, while Labour relies on millions of individual trade unionists who pay the political levy. Early in his leadership Tony Blair thanked the unions for sticking with the party when fair-weather friends deserted. Without them Labour could have gone under, and that was true again when he saddled the party with millions of pounds of secret debt before leaving office. Funding from trade unionists, with each individual contributing a few pounds a year, is clean compared with that from non-dom tycoons, and Labour should say so with pride.

And fifth, it needs public unity. The Tories were split over Europe, with John Major's "bastards" out of control. During the

1970s and 1980s Labour were seen as divided over almost everything. Chancellor Denis Healey was heckled at the party conference and battles broke out in the 1981 deputy leadership contest, described by Tony Benn, apparently without irony, as a healing process. But these days the members are loyal to a fault. They air disagreements over policy or doubts about the leadership in private, not on prime-time TV. They were let down by the plotters who destabilised successive leaders and attacked their comrades in the media, and by those Labour MPs who milked the expenses system and ex-ministers who sold themselves to the highest bidder.

The Rise and Fall of New Labour

Whatever happened later, Tony Blair's achievements in reviving Labour should never be underestimated. The party's base – manufacturing industry, trade union members, council tenants – shrank through the Thatcher/Major years, and gaining new support in the aspirational classes and in the south became essential. He neutralised the right-wing media by wooing Rupert Murdoch and took head-on the accusations of economic incompetence, thraldom to the trade unions, weakness on defence, sympathy for criminals over victims, and tolerance of benefit fraud. New Labour would be tough on crime and tough on the causes of crime, make responsibilities as important as rights, and stick to tight Tory spending limits. He attracted financial support from business as well as from traditional sources, and income from membership soared.

Tony Blair also imposed discipline on the party, reining in the activists and taking arguments out of the public eye. Indeed throughout his leadership, he defined himself against the party which he led, and against its past. This, and the birth of New Labour, were epitomised in changing clause IV of the constitution, replacing "common ownership of the means of production, distribution and exchange", with "a community in which power, wealth and opportunity are in the hands of the many, not the few". He could have lost the battle. In the run-up to the 1995 special conference it became clear that where activist general committees made the decision, constituencies mostly opposed change, while those which balloted members supported it overwhelmingly. Similarly trade union general secretaries were mandated by their political committees, against their mass membership, to vote for rejection. But the push towards one-member-one-vote won the day for Tony Blair, and the drama thrust New Labour and its leader into the public eye.

The clause IV experience reinforced Tony Blair's view, forged in the internecine wars of the 1970s and 1980s, that the activists, including conference delegates, did not speak for ordinary members. However, he did not recognise how much of his support came from people who would have voted for anything, including the slaughter of the firstborn, to get a Labour government again. Members will forgive their leaders a great deal while they are winning, which is why David Cameron's backbenchers are currently so quiet. Interestingly Tony Blair's fondness for one-member-one-vote waned when it started producing the wrong answers, notably in preferring Rhodri Morgan for Welsh leader and Ken Livingstone for Mayor of London.

After the 1997 victory a new policy-making process called *Partnership in Power* deprived the annual conference of its ability to embarrass the leadership. Only a handful of resolutions were allowed onto the agenda. Instead the arguments would take place in private within the national policy forum, which was given rule-book status in 1997. Its 200-odd members come from all sections of the movement, though dissident voices are largely excluded. Meetings are held once or twice a year, mostly informal chats around pre-drafted papers, but once in each parliamentary term the basis for the next manifesto is hammered out in all-night sessions between union general secretaries and ministers, in a process which combines the worst aspects of conference compositing with opaqueness to ordinary members.

The conference became little more than a rubber stamp for unamendable policy documents and an audience for ministers. The carefully-choreographed parades of handpicked speakers were boring for both members and the media, and there is now little coverage except when something goes wrong. The removal of 82-year-old Walter Wolfgang for heckling Jack Straw would never have occupied two full days of press coverage if there had also been real debate, with votes, on health, education, crime, defence or housing.

Grassroots input was limited to sending resolutions and views to the centre, where they were supposed to feed into policy commissions which bring together ministers and national policy forum members. Unfortunately initial enthusiasm for local forums and wide-ranging discussion evaporated when contributions were rarely acknowledged, let alone answered. There was now no channel through which concerns could be passed up from the grassroots, and so the Labour Government no longer heard the danger signals. Members desperately tried to warn of the folly of the 75p pension rise in 2000 and abolition of the 10% tax band in 2008, and were fobbed off. Tony Blair was mistaken in assuming that the activists were always wrong.

There was also little scope for influencing general policy directions. Most members will accept compromise: elections cannot be won with Guardian readers alone. But forcing through cuts to lone-parent benefit, on the night when Tony Blair entertained Cool Britannia in Downing Street, shocked Labour to its core. Sizeable numbers who went along with rightward policy shifts out of pragmatism were disconcerted to find that for the Blairites they were articles of faith. As under the old Tories the private sector was too often seen as superior, and local government was distrusted as an alternative power base. Shamefully the income of those unable to find work fell in real terms through 13 years of Labour government, and too many coalition policies can lay claim to New Labour parentage.

Even on touchstone issues Labour hesitated: despite fighting the 1999 Eddisbury by-election on the slogan "vote Labour or the fox gets it", 700 hours of parliamentary time was spent on hunting with dogs, ending with a fudge which satisfied no-one. Scottish and Welsh devolution required extra referendums. And then there was Iraq, the war and its aftermath, and the warm relationship with George Bush. Members understand the need to deal with rightwing US presidents, just as they understand the need to reassure businessmen. They do not expect their leader to enjoy it. And the perils of supping with the rich were evident, starting with the Bernie Ecclestone affair during Tony Blair's honeymoon, and running through to the massive unauthorised loans in 2005. His legacy is a shoe-string operation, with staffing and services slashed, higher charges for local parties, greater demands on volunteers, and a funding mix which is less diverse and more reliant on trade unionists than ever.

What Next?

Looking forward, Ed Miliband does not need a clause IV moment, nor to prove his dominance against his own party. Labour should not disown its past: good things should be celebrated, and errors should be acknowledged and not repeated. Whether or not they voted for him, the grassroots are loyal. However they do expect him to build a team which can take on the Tories in parliament, and more importantly in public forums and in the media. Politics becomes ever more presidential, and at the next election Ed Miliband will be up against David Cameron and whoever is leading the Lib Dems by then. Members are desperate for visible, hard-hitting, articulate and effective leadership.

They also want to contribute their experience and ideas. The national policy forum is not only exclusive, but isolated and impotent even in its own terms. Before the 2010 election Ed Miliband made a point of discussing the draft manifesto with a wide range of stakeholders, but regrettably he has not carried this forward as leader. Instead there are more than 20 shadow cabinet review groups whose membership is hidden even from the national executive committee.

The papers are full of stories about Blue Labour and Ed Miliband's guru Lord Glasman, and Purple Labour, a project backed by disgruntled Davidites through their *Progress* magazine. Thousands of individuals inside and outside the party have filled in policy questionnaires and posted their thoughts on the website, along with feedback from local parties. Little of this is available to the forum representatives who are supposed to act as conduits between the grassroots and the centre, but who get their 'information' from media rumours like everyone else, and end up as bystanders rather than ambassadors.

Peter Hain's *Refounding Labour* consultation on party reform may come up with answers, but I fear that they will be to the wrong questions. Overwhelmingly members simply want someone to hear and understand what they are saying, and they want open, accountable processes instead of policy-making by elites. As a member of the NEC, Labour's so-called ruling body, I know less now about how policy is made than sixteen years ago, when as a first-time conference delegate and local activist I started looking for the elusive national policy forum. Whether or not Ed Miliband becomes prime minister, he has a once-in-a-lifetime opportunity to change the culture of the party away from secrecy and towards engagement, and it would be a tragedy to waste it.

The Rt Hon Lord Whitty of Camberwell

Reflections on Labour Votes and Social Democratic Philosophy

Lord Whitty was General Secretary of the Labour Party between 1985 and 1994, under Neil Kinnock, John Smith and Tony Blair. He then served as European Co-ordinator between 1994 and 1997, between 1997 and 2005 he served in the Government as a Minister in both the DETR and the newly formed DEFRA.

A s I write this article, the press and many colleagues in the party are being very critical of Ed Miliband for not yet having redefined an identity for the post 2010 Labour Party.

But I would contend that after the Labour Party's second heaviest defeat since the 1930s, it is right that the leadership should promote both a long hard look at our policies and a root-and-branch review of our party structure and organisation – the 'Refounding Labour' project. Nor do I share the impatience of those who argue that these processes are taking far too long and that we should by now have defined our position.

I concede that ideally some immediate challenges should have been met with a more clearly defined positioning of the Party in opposition than we have yet managed – these include some pretty major issues. How we explain our economic legacy and our strategy on the deficit for example or our attitude to public sector pensions or to electoral reform and reaction to the defeat in the Scottish elections. But in the end – important though those issues are – a party will only be credible on such issues if our approach is rooted in a credible overall positioning. It is this repositioning that the party needs to address. I for one believe the process started by Ed Miliband is the correct one. We have about 18 months under a new leader to achieve that repositioning – that is to say about eight months to go from the time of writing, i.e. by the spring of 2012.

We need to reposition ourselves both philosophically and electorally. Philosophy took a bit of a back seat during the Blair and Brown period. The era of both 'Old Labour' and 'New Labour' has passed along with the societal assumptions that they reflected. The New Labour assumption was that we could meet ever rising aspirations of a growing majority in terms of purchasing power and consumer satisfaction by ensuring markets function efficiently with a 'light touch' state acting only as tiller and safety net. In the wake of the financial crisis and the downsides of globalisation, (both economically and environmentally) that scenario is just as dead as the Old Labour one, which depended on class solidarity and a centralised state capable of taking on international private power, to deliver equality and prosperity to the many.

I simplify to the point of caricature. But the reality is that we need a much more profound reassessment than could ever be provided by the sound bites and petty factionalism of the Blair Brown era.

Labour's Lost Millions

On the electoral side we have yet to have a proper analysis of where Labour's support disappeared. As has been said we lost five million votes between 1997 and 2010; four million under Blair and one million under Brown. Where did they all go?

By far the most important of those losses was the two million who voted Labour in 1997 but no longer vote at all. This is a problem for all political parties but it hits the Labour Party far more seriously.

There are some early myths being run which would give rise to the wrong conclusions in terms of political strategy. It is asserted, mainly by the media and by those who purport – although not entirely accurately – to carry forward the Blairite torch, that Labour's main problem is that we lost the votes of those in Middle England who flocked to the party of Tony Blair, and that we need to focus primarily on regaining those votes and particularly in the South of England.

The actual statistics show a rather different, more complex story. Comparing the 2010 election with 2001 (probably a more 'normal' election than 1997). For example, apart from those not voting at all, the exit polls show that Labour lost more of its working class vote than its middle class vote.

Percentage Change in Labour Vote 2001/2010 by Social Class

	Men	Women
AB	-8	+1
C1	-11	-9
C2	-16	-23
DE	-20	-11

Labour lost a higher proportion of its 'Council Tenant' lead than its vote amongst mortgage holders

Percentage Change in Labour Lead over Conservatives 2001/2010

Owners outright	-10
Mortgaged	-2
Social Rented	-19
Private rented	-6

And Labour lost more men than women

Percentage Change in Labour Vote 2001/2010

Men	-16%
Women	- 9%
ALL	-12%

The above figures are all derived from Mori exit polls in 2001 and 2010.

On the geographical dimension, since 1997, Labour lost more of its vote in the so called 'heartlands' in the Midlands and the North of England and Wales than in the South.

Percentage Change in Labour Vote 1997/2010 by Region

London	-13
S East	-13
E&W Midlands	-17
Yorkshire	-17
Wales	-18
N East	-20

NB Scotland with a decline of only 3% was an exception
(until the Scottish Parliament elections)

In other words Labour lost proportionately more amongst its traditional strongholds than amongst those who may have switched to Labour since 1992.

Do not get me wrong. I am not drawing the opposite conclusion from these figures. We do have to win back significant southern and middle class support – even more so because the demographic and geographical balance of the population has shifted against Labour and this will be exaggerated in the redrawn boundaries after the Parliamentary Voting System and Constituencies Act 2011. But let us also understand that we have to bring back to Labour significant numbers of what was our 'core vote' – from failure to vote at all, from the Lib Dems, from the SNP and from the Far Right; and from the Tories too.

Who are Labour's 'core vote' and why did we lose so many of them over the period of Labour Government? By 'core vote' I am not relying on some romantic abstraction of a clear class identity. Put crudely, Labour's core vote consists of three main elements, and in different ways we managed to upset them all significantly at various points in the 13 years we were in government:

Traditional White Working Class, particularly male manual workers: For whom much was done in the early part of the Labour Government, such as the Minimum Wage and the level of state pensions – but who lost identity with Labour – often by default – as a result of the neglect of manufacturing, distancing from the unions, failure to deliver affordable housing for purchase or rent and the unacknowledged consequences of immigration policy on communities.

Liberal Professionals (particularly those working in public services): Many of whom were alienated by our public service reforms, and what often appeared to be our general disparagement of public service and public servants extolling the virtues of the private sector; and more specifically our policies on education, the health service and over-zealous security measures. In some cases they were also differentially by Iraq.

Ethnic Minorities who for the most part still backed Labour (and indeed saved many seats in 2010) but nowhere near as solidly as in 1997 and earlier. Mostly this reflects a degree of embourgeoisement leading to voting eclecticism – as it had earlier with the Jewish and Irish vote. However, the largest and until then most consistently supportive and best organised minority groups – the Muslims deserted significantly in 2005 over Iraq and perceived anti-Muslim security and international policies – did not vote or switched to the Lib Dems and Respect – though many returned in 2010.

It seems bizarre to have alienated so comprehensively substantial elements of three main parts of our core vote. This is not to say that all the policies that caused this alienation were failures or misdirected. Some policies I supported and some I did not. But there are electoral consequences both of particular policies and of general neglect. The chipping away at our base support has proved deeply damaging. The party needs to re-establish relevance and identity with these groups.

Those who argue that these changes in voting patterns are just part of a general breakdown of tribal voting, as class definitions become more complex, are only partly right. Class divisions and identities are indeed much more complicated than in the 1950s or even 1980s, but there are clear group behaviours still present in society, which include psephological behaviours. People need political movements with whom they can generally identify in terms of style and of overall philosophy; at the moment Labour does not have that.

The Philosophy of Social Democracy
European Social Democracy has had a bad decade. Many

including me, would have predicted that the collapse of communism in the nineties and the near collapse of financial capitalism in the late noughties ought to have led to a hegemonic position for social democracy amongst electorates. The hour of social democracy should have come! In fact we have gone backwards. In 1997, after the victories of Blair in the UK and Jospin in France in that spring, of the then 15 states of the EU, two thirds were governed by social democrats, excluding Spain – who had only just lost power. By mid 2011 there remained three – Portugal has already gone and Greece and Spain are likely to be removed, by dint of being in power at the point of the great financial collapse, and the subsequent Euro crisis. There are many differences between social democrats in each of these EU countries and differences in the electoral culture and electoral cycles. The lack of cohesion amongst social democratic parties in Europe has not helped – for which in part, I blame Tony Blair who tended to dismiss French and even Nordic social democrats as stuck in the past. Either way social democracy needs a refreshed philosophical positioning and a renewed electoral strategy.

I am not a political philosopher myself and am not here going to spell out a total philosophy for the next generation of social democratic leaders. I simply identify two strands which had been central to the social democratic approach, and need redefining for the modern more complex age.

They are:

Commitment to Equality of Outcome: In all policies we need to focus again on great equality as being a desirable outcome

The Role of the State: The state, in its many forms needs to be seen as one of many levers but still the main instrument of achieving that greater equality of outcome

Greater Equality as an Objective

The increasing inequality under Thatcher continued at only a slightly slower rate across 13 years of Labour. The most widely accepted comparative measure of inequality – the Gini coefficient – shows the UK in the last 20 years has gone from being one of the most equal societies to one of the least.

And despite substantial programmes of redistribution under New Labour – such as the tax credit system, or of social capital such as Sure Start. The period of Labour Government saw some seriously depressing outturns in terms of inequality.

1998/9 to 2008/9

	Change in Real Income %	Share of Growth %
Poorest Decile	- 12	0
2nd Decile	+25	4
3rd Decile	+29	5
4th Decile	+26	6
5th Decile	+24	7
6th Decile	+33	8
7th Decile	+22	9
8th Decile	+23	10
9th Decile	+23	13
Richest Decile	+37	40

Moreover, for the topmost 1%, the increase was much greater and not just amongst hedge funders and oligarchs. In many companies the CEO was earning 200 times as much as the lowest grades when most public opinion surveys show that an acceptable level would be much less than 20 times. Unfortunately this escalation and leapfrogging of senior executive salaries also infected the public sector.

Nor was this inequality compensated for by greater social mobility. Even the Coalition have realised that Britain's social mobility is very limited compared to other advanced economies (although similar to the United States) and getting worse not better. Much of this was blamed on globalisation – as if in return for the benefits of globalisation we had to accept boardroom salaries reflecting those paid in Houston, Texas whilst wages for cleaners reflecting those in Vietnam.

A central part of any new plank for strategy of the post New Labour Party has to be reversing this corrosive trend to greater inequality.

Role of the State

If the objective is greater equality then the main instrument is the state. However over this period just as inequality grew and social mobility almost ground to a halt there was a concerted attack on the legitimacy of the use of the state to offset economic inequality and unfairness.

There were many highly desirable interventions; a series of important measures to proscribe behaviour based on discrimination – culminating in the Equalities Act. The raising of the real value of pensions; and the principle of the tax credit system, were in differing ways designed to blunt the effects of inequality. But the use of the state as an instrument of redistribution was at best down played and at times denied in policy making.

Of course the nature of the state is also important. Under Thatcher and Major, and reinforced under Blair and Brown, the state became too centralised, too intrusive and insufficiently accountable. That too needs to be addressed – not to restrict the state to limited spheres but to ensure its operations are transparent and accountable. In particular, with a strong role for the local state – our local government structure whose legitimacy was undermined to an even greater extent in those years with a combined onslaught from Whitehall, the media and nimbyism. The localism agenda of the Coalition seems more inclined to by-pass democratic local structures.

The next stage of strategy for social democracy in Britain and Europe must see the reinstallation of the aim of greater equality as key to our political strategy, and the primacy of the state and local government as instruments towards that policy.

Two Key Policy Areas as Examples

I am not going to go through the whole gamut of policy areas but briefly just pick two, in which I am interested and where the issue of equality of outcome and the issue of the role of the state are important. One is very close to the individual citizen; one is apparently much more remote and global: Housing and Climate Change.

Housing

We now have the lowest level of new build houses since the 1920s, 4 million on social housing lists, 3 million families overcrowded and countless more young people living at home; we have the average age for gaining a mortgage shifting from late 20s to 37 going on 40. As credit dries up, demand for deposits becomes prohibitive and in areas of high housing stress, both house prices and private rents are soaring, particularly but not exclusively in the South East. Low interest rates have cushioned life for those who have been on a mortgage for more than ten years but that will not last. Labour's main pre-occupation in office was pitching ever higher targets for home ownership, shifting social housing stock away from councils to less accountable bodies and moving towards the marketising of social rents subsidised by increasing Housing Benefit, trying various commendable but largely unsuccessful passerelle schemes for transfer from rent to mortgage, and providing tax inducements for buy to let. The fact is that all sectors of the housing market have ended up as dysfunctional due to a combination of the credit crunch and misguided policies. We have to think again.

Housing is rapidly moving up the political agenda and needs to be seen as a priority responsibility for both national and local government. The atomised society in which we now live, with formation and reformation of households means we need a housing strategy that combines security and flexibility.

We need new thinking outside of the box of separate policies for social, private rented and owner occupation. We need both new build to high environmental standards and better utilisation and refurbishment of our existing housing stock. That requires new forms of finance for all sectors.

Housing has not only individual resonance but also wider social implications. We must avoid outcomes that increase social and ethnic polarisation in housing and aim to create neighbourhoods of mixed incomes and mixed tenure. Housing is a hugely important and strategic mighty task for policy makers in this review.

Climate Change

At the global end of the scale, on the face of it the last Labour Government – thanks not least to the Miliband brothers – left us in a good place for tackling what in the end may be the biggest problem of all, mitigating and adapting to climate change. We have inherited a lead position in international negotiations and a clear framework under the Climate Change Act.

Regrettably the combination of inadequate measures, increased climate change scepticism and diversion of both political and public attention to the financial crisis, has meant that promise is not being delivered. Thankfully, for the moment there remains some cross party agreement, at least in principle here. The Labour Party needs to play its part in developing effective measures to reduce fossil fuel consumption through financial instruments, supporting radical new technology and encouraging major individual and corporate behaviour change.

Unfortunately many of the measures so far in place put the cost of mitigating and adapting onto the world's poor – both in developed and emerging economies through energy pricing and through patterns of trade. Climate Change strategies that do not depend on further inequality are desperately needed. Again a major task for Labour in our policy review, and there are many more.

The Party Itself

To tackle the electoral challenge and grapple with these daunting policy issues the Refounding Labour project needs to be radical. Before the General Election, our membership was at its lowest ever and activism and engagement within that membership at best patchy. We are neither a fighting electoral machine nor a place for the ferment of ideas; we need to be both. Our finances and those of the trade unions in their political funds are not in good shape and may well be attacked by the Coalition Government through political funding legislation.

Again I do not have a prescription in detail. But the project needs to deliver at least the following: refocusing the party membership and resources at levels where politics mean something to people, and where we can run a viable size of organisation – to me this means focussing on local government level organisation, increasing membership and supporters, reaching a new settlement between the party and the unions on the constitutional structure; identifying new sources of finance which do not depend on large donations from a few people; and turning the Policy Forum process into something closer to the original concept with meaningful engagement for our members and beyond.

Just a few of the tasks for our Labour Leadership to deliver. No-one said it was going to be easy.

Dr. Rupa Huq

The Path Back to Power is a Suburban One

Rupa is a senior lecturer in Sociology at Kingston University. Her first book "Beyond Subculture: Pop, Youth and Identity in a Post-Colonial World" was shortlisted for the British Sociological Association's Philip Abrams Memorial Prize. Her forthcoming book "Utopia on the Edge: making sense of suburbia in the age of insecurity" will be published in 2012.She is a columnist for Tribune magazine.

This chapter considers the political significance of contemporary UK suburbia. The suburbs are where most British people live, but they have only relatively recently attracted political interest. Boris Johnson's successful 2008 London Mayoral campaign, Labour post mortems after the 2010 General Election (e.g. Ed Miliband's concept of the "squeezed middle", the Policy Exchange report *Southern Discomfort Again*) and Nick Clegg's "alarm clock Britain" all recognise the extent to which suburban voters and their concerns will be the key to electoral success after New Labour.

Changing Values and Situations

In Anglo-Saxon parlance suburbs – close to the city but distinct from it, boasting the benefits of general salubriousness and greenery – evoke aspiration and progress, security and social respectability, even if they have long been maligned by critics for social and architectural monotony. Stereotypically seen as middle class and "safe", suburbs were built in optimism on the principle of defensible space in both their owner-occupier and social housing "homes fit for heroes" versions; their great expansion was in the inter-war years of the 1930s. Yet as old models of hidebound class fragment in the face of occupational restructuring and ethnic diversity, arguably *insecurity* characterises modern times: polling shows that immigration and fear of crime are top suburban fears. Added to this are economic and environmental instability and the spectre of domestic terrorism. All of these are arguments for a rethinking of suburbia, which in the twenty-first century is increasingly culturally diverse, with a built environment often suffering from un-let retail units where an ageing and anxious population reside.

How should the centre left respond? Suburban values embody materialism: private house builders marketed suburban living as a consumer choice in contrast to the constraint of remaining in the decaying city. Yet suburbs no longer fit the traditional template of dormitory towns for a male breadwinning city-centre workforce with attendant housewives. The dual earner household is the norm and networked society allows more working from home. Old structures have fractured: trade union membership has been in long term decline, the public sector is set to contract and the old politics of redistribution has been supplemented with the new left concerns like the struggle of minorities who fight for recognition. David Cameron has continued the Conservative tradition championing suburban values of moralism and property ownership (e.g. Thatcher's granting council tenants the right to purchase their homes) in promising tax-breaks for the married and changes to inheritance tax. The claim "we're all in this together" from George Osborne, a Tory of considerable means, has been contradicted with a lack of action on banker's bonuses and the fact that women will be hardest hit by Conservative spending cuts including child benefit changes.

Other traditional suburban identifications are also in flux. Rising rates of divorce and reconstituted households help the property market remain dynamic rendering the once suburban cornerstone of the nuclear family less dominant. Increasing lifespans make social care a key concern in suburbia. It seems the British are less and less a nation of "joiners" too – church attendance has since fallen in an age of rationalism, science and progress, although faith school admissions criteria has sustained congregations to an extent. Social class is less easily definable than before requiring new classificatory models. Occupational groupings are more fluid than before with indeterminate service sector jobs (eg call centre staff) difficult to place in the old white collar/blue collar binary. However the parentage and postcode of your birth places a defining role in future life-chances even if politicians including John Major (classless society) and croquet-playing John Prescott (we are all middle class now) have indicated that class struggle is an anachronistic relic of the past.

British governments have followed a consensus in restricting immigration policy while allowing ex-colonial subjects the vote which has made minorities an electoral bloc to woo rather than simply demonise. Suburbs are associated with "white flight", where those who could get out did. One could coin the concept "brown flight" for the embourgeoisement and suburbanisation of Labour-voting ethnic minorities along familiar arterial roads and transport links e.g. African Caribbeans from inner city Brixton to suburban Croydon. Suburbia has been the point of arrival for others e.g. South Koreans in New Malden in outer South London. Ethnic votes have helped Labour e.g. in the once-safe Tory constituencies of Harrow West or Brent North favoured by affluent Indians. Up north frustrations over structural decline amongst Pakistani and Bangladeshi communities stoked by BNP provocation flared into riots in Bradford, Burnley and Oldham into 2001. Ironically the jobs that the now parents or grandparents who came from Sylhet or the Punjab to the UK to do in these former cotton mill-towns have since been outsourced back to the subcontinent.

Some of the structural features common to the northern towns of the 2001 disturbances are also present in the south. Luton is the base of the English Defence League formed to oppose Islam. It was where the failed Stockholm terror-plot was based and where the 2005 7/7 London bombers set out from. It was once considered to be a town outside London but has become a de facto suburb of it due to the capital's expanded commuting pull. Luton's biggest employer Vauxhall, once a thriving car plant allowing employees of different ethnic and religious backgrounds to mix on the production line, now has a dramatically shrunken workforce. Economic woes and an adjustment to de-industrialisation feed simmering tension. Barking and Dagenham a couple of boroughs east of London's financial district similarly suffered after its major employer, Ford, largely withdrew. The area has become popular with African settlers often moving from inner London boroughs in the same way as the classic sociological work *Family and Kinship in East London* documented east-end diaspora in the 1960s. Disenchantment by the white electorate was orchestrated in the 2006 local elections where the BNP became the second biggest force on the local council. One thing that radical Islam, the BNP and EDL all embody is lessening faith with mainstream politics.

Prospects for Labour and Social Democracy in Suburbia

Although opposition is a new phenomenon to many of the New Labour generation, the root-and-branch policy review underway allows Ed Miliband the opportunity to fashion a strong manifesto with a clear message for the next election. It is said that parties campaign in poetry but govern in prose. Electoral logic needs the resultant policies to appeal to mainstream voters in marginal, often suburban, seats without alienating traditional core Labour supporters. A convincing narrative has to be presented to the electorate without sacrificing principle. Labour has tapped into suburban values in recent years by repeatedly emphasising "hard working families" but their 2010 offer "A Future Fair For All" did not appeal to voters' base instincts as nakedly as the Conservatives' policy of changes to inheritance tax and were not as easily graspable as its 1997 election pledges: targets that were universally popular that could be fitted on a calling-card. Equal access to life-chances for all could look as if it is advocating a process of "levelling down" to the status conscious of suburbia. Signals that the new leadership considers the pre-emptive "liberal interventionism" rationale of the Iraq invasion mistaken could rebuild bridges with those that deserted Labour after 2005 and win back lost seats eg in the Manchester suburb of Withington. The collapse of credibility attached to monetarism as an economic philosophy offers an opportunity to build a new economic policy focusing less on speculative asset bubbles like the housing market and more on better regulation of financial services to curb casino capitalism bankers. A new programme could include employee share options. It should not ignore the politics of aspiration. It should address affordable housing with solutions, not only that of council housing but by reforming expensive shared equity schemes (often flats unsuitable as family sized homes) and recognising the natural impulse of home-ownership. A welfare programme must be devised where the benefits system makes work pay.

The Conservatives "big idea" the small state "big society" whereby citizens become consumers exercising autonomy in public services needs to be exposed as a dangerous dogma-driven cover for cuts. Looser community politics could be a beneficiary of the malaise surrounding traditional politics – the Obama Presidential campaign successfully mobilised voters by the principles of community organisation. Labour effectively united communities in the 2010 local elections when the BNP lost all of its seats on the Barking and Dagenham council and its media-courting leader Nick Griffin failed to take the parliamentary seat there working with the TUC supported pressure group "Hope Not Hate". This rainbow alliance from inside and outside the party could be a possible model for moving forward. Labour also has a strong local government presence which it needs to build on. May 2010 saw impressive Labour local electoral performance with gains in suburbs including Ealing and Harrow. These councils need to now propagate responsible financial stewardship in tough times to popularise the Labour brand in the country. It is also a mistake to take any voters for granted: the settled UK Asian community often have the most anti-immigration stances. Conservative pandering to social conservatism e.g. in the moralism of proposing tax breaks for marriage, could well be a misjudgement when opinion polling has showed that attitudes once thought to be "socially liberal" are now more widespread, increasingly becoming "the norm" (Reeves 2007) e.g. tolerance of homosexuality. Indeed before their recession-induced about-turn the Conservatives had advocated sticking to Labour's spending plans in much the same way as New Labour pledged to retain Tory targets in its first two years of office, suggesting that social democracy has intellectually "won".

The longstanding gulf between people and the authorities has occurred over time and therefore will not be solved over night. Labour needs to channel recent activism e.g. opposition to coalition cuts and student protestors into ballot box results. David Cameron announced at the end of 2010 that the Government would start collating statistics on happiness and national well-being. Labour needs to demonstrate to voters that it is "on their side" and working with communities i.e. doing things *with* people and *for* people rather than *to* them. The idea of citizenship is a relatively new one in the UK but could be one area that Labour could make its own. During the last parliament it was the Conservatives who opposed Labour legislation on detaining pre-trial suspects without charge and compulsory ID cards with libertarian right-wingers, e.g. David Davis MP, arguing that national security was being used as a cover for eroding civil liberties. Now that the coalition is reneging on promises in this area e.g. the pledge to abolish control orders, this is territory that Labour should move in on. At all times Labour should not forget that it is about defending society's weakest but the aspiring classes should not be ignored.

From 1997 – 2005 Labour asserted itself as the natural party of government, which it failed to do in 2010. To regain power it needs to mobilise different groups including suburbanites, women, younger voters and left intellectuals as well as its stereotypical natural voters of the industrial heartlands. There needs to be a reconsideration of cohesive communities as a goal for everyone rather than something just affecting various "other people" elsewhere. Indeed despite unprecedented economic crises and the most unpopular Prime Minister since polling began and the Ashcroft millions, Labour was able to deny Cameron overall victory in 2010. Labour needs to expose Nick Clegg, Vince Cable, Danny Alexander et al as unprincipled, duplicitous and opportunist. Their readiness to do anything to get into power and their bums on the seats of ministerial Priuses at national level is only a mirror of how they have operated in local government for years.

Conclusion

Now more than ever before it is the suburbs that will be the most decisive battleground in deciding the next election outcome by which time the fragility of the shaky coalition as well as the extent of the cuts will be clearer. Suburbia however needs to be reconstructed from clichés[1] as a vibrant place of possibilities rather than the neither-here-nor-there territory it has long been relegated to. Modernity has taken its toll in the suburbs. The promised utopia of cool Britannia and its attendant urban regeneration with city centre pedestrianisation with a dash of greenery has barely touched many areas of the city limits or worse still has adversely affected them leaving a trail of empty retail units engendering suburban decay to the point that Boris Johnson's promised Outer London Commission gimmick was able to exploit suburban discontent. Labour needs to match and better this. Rather than

Labour carrying associations of being overly in thrall to big business, finance capital and multinational-led globalisation, its strength in local government offers Labour councils a chance to show small businesses that it is on their side by incentivising spending locally. Localism can still be a cause championed even if we are tied to international agreements.

Values reflect times and circumstances. The credit search company Experian recently found that 57% of Middle Britain struggle to find enough hours in the day to manage life. The term "Risk Society" of Ulrich Beck (1992) describes individualism and choice triumphing over old bonds but structuring frameworks remain. In France, a country that like the UK also has been dealing with the stresses of postcolonialism, the term "l'insecurité" has been part of political dialogue since the 1990s referring to a clutch of issues including immigration, unemployment and law and order matters. More recently it seems that we are constantly told we are in an age of uncertainty (e.g. Lott 2009, McGhee 2010). Such complexity could explain the solace sought in harking back to simpler times, in the popularity of television costume drama (the phenomenally successful stately-home tale *Downton Abbey*) and even returning to the land via social networking (the Facebook application Farmville).

Suburbia is a fraught territory composed of multiple, overlapping and fundamentally contested cultures. Old institutions (e.g. church, state, parliament, party, union etc) may hold less sway with the suburban voter or British resident/citizen/subject at large but this is a reality to be accepted and worked with rather than a state of affairs to be bewailed. Class consciousness too seems questionable as a left totem when workers have largely become customer-consumers. Suburbs built to appeal to traditionalism, as seen in their nostalgic architecture, now embody modernity. They are inhabited by diverse people, with multifaceted identities negotiating increasingly atomised and time-poor lives. Shoe-horning them into constructed categories in a quest to find "what people can unite around" seems to be a little forced when genuine community cohesion is more likely to be forged rather than forced. Perhaps the mistake is to seek one banner under which Britain's diverse multi-faceted mosaic can all unproblematically unite around.

By 2014 we will be 18 years away from Blair's high watermark of 1997: the same distance that 1997 was from 1979. Fighting the next election on prescriptions from then would be deeply misguided. So what certainties can be relied on in an age of insecurity? With the economic crisis exposing the limits of untrammelled turbo-capitalism worldwide, Labour now has an opportunity free from the strains of office to develop a programme based on centre-left values to present to the electorate when the time comes, rather than simply promising more of the same. "The economy (stupid)" matters but not exclusively at the expense of culture. For electoral purposes suburban dwellers should not all be seen as an undifferentiated mass. Britain's former imperial possessions and post-war immigration have changed the face of suburbia irrevocably. Global uncertainty itself should not be feared but accepted and negotiated; perhaps the reason that it has perplexed as it has is because in normal peacetime conditions life had become *too* predictable, even boring. Winston Churchill once claimed "Without a measureless and perpetual uncertainty, the drama of human life would be destroyed." Contested terms like the neither-here-nor-there territory of "suburbia" or difficult to pin down "age of insecurity" might be outside policy-makers' theoretical comfort zones but they need addressing head on by Labour to avoid the next General Election going the same way as the last one.

Tony Lloyd MP

In Search of Labour's Big Idea

Tony Lloyd was first elected to Parliament in the 1983 General Election. He is currently the Chairman of the Parliamentary Labour Party, and serves as Chair of the Trade Union Group of Labour MPs.

It is necessary that Labour, out of power after years in government, engages in a process of self-analysis. Unless we demand the luxury of insisting that the electorate got it wrong, without trashing the enormous achievements of Labour in government, we have to look at what we didn't get right. That process must ask us to look not just to policy but to our tradition and to align them with the present. Labour's tradition, like that of most radical parties across the world, was clearly Utopian. Labour was a bold party holding out a vision of society, not as it was, but as it could be.

Yet wherever we look, the radical left over recent decades has lost confidence. Electoral politics seemingly demands that we choose managerial politics, where we campaign as the better managers of government, mainly of the economy and of public services, over the visionary politics of our past which our instincts prefer. Reality says that there is inevitable compromise between these two poles. However, it is not just reactionary ideologues who think that New Labour's embarrassment at its old friends, the role of the state, our trade union base and its embracing of "business-friendly" solutions, had unfortunate consequences.

"Business-friendly" became an over-closeness not to business generally – a perfectly sensible place to be – but rather to that increasingly powerful clutch of global corporations and, as we saw with the NewsCorp saga, it's most senior managers. The economy was distorted as we put the interests of the financial corporations ahead of those of activities like manufacturing or tourism with their greater capacity to create broad-based wealth and employment. And our politics were distorted as we did the same with the media.

We undervalued the role of the trade unions, preferring them rather like the drunken old uncle, to be tolerated but kept out of the way. In reality when it came to many political decisions for the Labour leadership and government, the trade unions were part of the solution. Consider, for example, the way public-sector pensions were dealt with when sympathetic government ministers negotiated in good faith with the unions, solutions were found without acrimony.

It was much harder for the public to see what Labour stood for at the end of our period in government. Too many Labour voters and ex-voters were not sure what Labour's ambitions were and who would be their beneficiaries. Ed Miliband is right to identify the squeezed middle as disillusioned but it went deeper than the economy or even Iraq.

Compare that uncertainty to Labour's historic victories. Labour won in '45, '64 and '97 by being very different from the Conservatives we replaced. Each of those governments delivered on an agenda that modernised the Britain of its era. Remember the wave of enthusiasm for change in 1997 which let Labour begin its radical early years with a commitment to full employment, the minimum wage, Gordon Brown's campaign against child poverty, a commitment to increasing aid to 0.7% of GDP, and the commitment to an Equal Opportunities Britain. All that was done within the confines of budgets set by the outgoing Tories. The Labour government changed our country for the better.

And now in Opposition again, we discover how hard it is to make our voice heard. So we look forward to the next general election, after a period where inevitably the coalition government dominates the agenda. It is hard to believe we can win that election on minimalist politics where we seek only to position ourselves around the coalition's policies with a little bit more here or a little less there. We can only succeed in so far as they are deemed to have failed on the agenda that they will set and themselves constantly re-set. They are in the serious business of lowering public expectations just as the Thatcher-Major governments did in the 1980s and 1990s. And a public intimidated by the constant repetition of the simple refrain that it's Labour's fault, will doubt our capacity to achieve more than the David Cameron Tories, to whom they will have become accustomed and who will be seen as the safe option.

So Labour has to be bold and set a better vision of what Britain and the world can be.

The Shrinking State or the Power of the State

Even amongst some influential Labour figures, David Cameron's 'Big Society' is seen as offering a political challenge we need to copy. The public is underwhelmed by it. Yet it most certainly does offer a political challenge not just to Labour but to society as a whole. For the 'Big Society' in Conservative hands – even in its most benign form – is about shrinking the power of the state.

Even if we forget the likelihood that underfunded voluntary organisations are doomed to fail, possibly to be replaced, in the absence of dismantled public institutions, by the private sector, the shrinking of the power of the state is exactly the wrong direction of travel for modern Britain and the world.

Britain has a huge range of voluntary and third sector organisations like the Scouts, London Citizens, the WI, the churches and religious organisations and more, along with probably the most extensive independent NGO community in the world. And of enormous importance are our free trade unions. All these bodies would welcome a greater constructive role in society. The brutal reality is that every one of these would not be strengthened but weakened by a partnership with a smaller, enfeebled state.

A Labour 'Big Society' has at its very heart the recognition of the power of collective action through all of the organisations like those outlined above but able to work with, influence and sometimes criticise the actions of the biggest of all collective actors, all of us working together through the power of state action. So what is this 'state' that is so feared and demonised by the Tories? It is no more or less than the power of us all acting together, but democratically elected and ultimately accountable, in ways that no corporation ever can be.

Let us admit that a general election fought on the power of state action versus the shrinking state would drive the public to levels of boredom not achieved even by John Major.

However, if Labour were to deny the choice to our nation of using of the power of the state in ways we have not recently exploited, we would fail in addressing the problems which we are likely to face in government.

So what will Labour inherit in government?

No one knows whether the coalition will make it all the way through to 2015 or whether the Tories will find reasons to abandon the Lib Dems before then. Either way Labour will face (some of) the following problems.

An under-performing economy will lack the capacity to generate the resource base for any major new short-term investments either economically or socially.

Unemployment seems likely once again to be on the up, especially in those traditional areas of high unemployment.

The trade unions will naturally come under pressure from their own members to take action to defend what can be defended. Both wings of the coalition will unite in talking about and possibly seeking to restrict the actions of those unions.

Our public services will be smaller, demoralised and not necessarily able to deliver what society expects of them. Some, especially the NHS, may already have been broken up, reducing capacity to offer a truly national public service. Other services, under-financed and under-regulated, may go the way of Southern Cross (a private operator which provided residential care for the elderly and recently went bust) or Winterbourne View (where vulnerable residents were treated brutally by those charged with their care).

In vital industries like rail, we will see the public sector (through subsidy) or the public (through fare hikes) continue to pour money in to keep private companies afloat and the public, not the private sector, will carry on bearing all the risk but the private sector will carry off any profit.

The giant corporations, energy companies, the banks and the like will continue to cock a snoop at the public and the high-pay/high bonus culture will be justified as being in the national interest. The genuinely wealth-spreading and employment-creating parts of the economy will be just as damaged by high energy costs and lack of access to finance as the general public.

Pension policy and care for the elderly will be targeted as a problem for society as the age profile of society grows older, not instead as an affordable social obligation – albeit one involving political choice. Rising house prices, conversely, will be seen as a good thing despite the fact that young people will be priced out of the housing market until they are much older than before. In practice those rising prices represent a transfer from younger generations of would be home-owners to the older generation of owners.

Access to justice, a fundamental in a properly functioning society, will be restricted to the very rich and to that diminishing group still able to access legal aid. The conman, the bully, the bad employer, the Rachman landlord and the unscrupulous will relish the prospect.

A divided Britain with a decreasing sense of common purpose and identity, will see the have-nots, demoralised and resentful, tempted by the BNP and their like.

And Corporate Britain will roll on unassailable, its beneficiaries operating without restraint, constraint or meaningful apology.

This is, of course, a very bleak picture of Britain that many may not recognise or choose to recognise and it may not all come to pass. What is certain is that some of this will take place, indeed already is doing so.

So what should Labour be and do?
It would be stupid to trash all of Labour's period in government in order to re-assess what modern Labour is all about. It isn't necessary to retreat into some cosy view of Labour's history to insist that "Labour is at its best when it is Labour" and that we should still be informed by our values, traditional or modern.

Labour's values comprise many legitimate strands; committed to strengthening the right to collective action, we are on the side of the powerless, we are challenging of those who hold unaccountable power, we are internationalist, egalitarian, we are libertarian whilst recognising the right of the community to limit excessive individualism, we are anti-racist, and, of course, 'for the many, not the few'. In the world a Labour government is likely to confront, those are exactly the right values to inform our policy choice. At home we need to use the power of democratically elected government, whether national or local, to advance the interests of the whole nation.

We should be proud of the support Labour gave in government to those most in need, whether in early years through Sure Start or by funding health and education in a way that was good for all but helped the most needy. The welfare state does require a relationship insisting on responsibility as well as offering rights but in a decent society we don't pay in only in order to take out, instead the strong support the less strong because that is what social cohesion is all about. And together we are stronger than apart.

Labour rightly looked at developing a National Care Service when we were in office. That and decisions about the affordability of pensions are consciously political choices. We should not be bound by the choices of this coalition because dignity in old age or at a time of vulnerability should be an ambition Labour wants to espouse, even if we cannot achieve everything immediately.

High and enduring levels of employment should once again be a key goal. We need long-term strategies for investment in skills training, science and engineering research and development. We should visit again some of the ideas like a national investment bank to overcome the shortcomings of the present financial system, especially in not lending to innovative manufacturers. And we should look at training levies for those who refuse to train.

The nationalisation of the failed banks on the one hand, or the market failure of groups like Southern Cross should tell us that the private sector cannot hand over the economic Holy Grail so where appropriate we should look to the public sector not to underwrite market failure but to provide services directly. Social housing, provision of services for the elderly become obvious, and there is a strong and arguable case that the present franchising arrangements for the rail system should be gradually ended and replaced by public provision.

Regulation has got to be redefined. Labour grew afraid of the argument that regulation was red-tape and the consequences were a Quality Services Commission which allowed the vulnerable to be brutalised at Winterbourne House. Britain's energy suppliers, a self-serving oligopoly, act unconstrained by the energy regulator and ratchet up prices at every opportunity, charging the highest price to those least able to afford it. Our media was out of real control with an industry-comfy Press Complaints Council. Our bankers continue with a bonus culture which sickens people, and they still do not do the basic job of bankers, of taking some risk whilst lending to companies and individuals who need and can use that lending. Our regulators have to be given independence, a duty to serve the wider public and real teeth to alter behaviour.

The culture of high pay is socially and morally unacceptable and of no great value to the economy. We need a High-Pay Commission which has the capacity to develop policies and the clout to implement them to change the culture of greed. A commission should at least look at maximum differentials between top pay and the average, at employee representation on remuneration committees, and at the need for public reporting. It could conclude we need statutory limits on high pay.

The culture of low pay for women relative to men is still too strong and that needs equally strong action. Company reporting of equal opportunity policies would be a start.

And we do need to recognise the positive role of strong trade unions. Issues like pension negotiations, fair and equal pay, dealing with demoralised workforces and industrial relations generally are all better when trade unions are involved. But the trade unions have a much wider capacity to involve their members and engage in the debate about what kind of society we should be. No one argues they are the only source of wisdom in Britain but few other structures have their reach in numbers or their democratic structures. Some of the legal constraints that they have had to put up with are unfair and jeopardise their ability to play a constructive role at all.

Labour's commitment to equality of opportunity was part of a wider social change but we are not where we should be yet. Britain is not an intolerant place but we have no future unless all of our citizens feel secure. Equal pay, as discussed above, is still too real but so too is discrimination on grounds of race or sexuality. Government shouldn't be afraid to challenge these prejudices. And high on that list is being clear when immigration is in all of our interest, and refusing to run an immigration policy based on the fear of racism. On the other hand we do need to recognise that social harmony depends on communities living together and that means social effort in those parts of Britain where change has been sharpest. It seems obvious, for example, that we should re-establish English language classes for those who don't speak English, especially for women with children at school.

At the international level, the European Union is a natural place to start. The recent debate on the EU has focussed on the Euro and whilst few would argue for Britain's membership of that, we need to re-define a positive attitude to the EU. We need a Social Europe not just a Market Europe, a Europe committed to full employment and to a proper balance between a dynamic market and the rights and needs of those who work and live here, and one which helps constrain the global corporation. We should join with those who share that view.

Britain is stronger and more influential if that Social Europe uses its influence on the world stage. It is self-interest as well as being morally right that we work for a more equal world. That means, for example, the EU's preoccupation with free trade deals at the WTO to increase world trade, however worthwhile for advanced economies, should recognise that developing countries need some protection against economic exploitation by the more powerful economies. It also means the human rights we take for granted should be supported globally by collective EU action.

But the enormous existential threats to human existence as we know it, global warming, the environmental threat to our oceans, weapons of mass-destruction, all require international solutions. Those solutions are more likely to be forthcoming if we recognise we really are all in it together. Some of those need strengthened global structures, especially the United Nations. But we need to work with the like-minded and to campaign for the politics of change and help change minds globally. The coalition of the willing should not be something only put together for military campaigns.

Conclusion

Labour will face real challenges in government, very different from those in the late 1990s.

Britain is different and the world is different. It is not ironic that whilst Labour's values were part of what made Britain better under the last Labour government, those same values are now vital if we are to address Britain's challenges and to build a global politics which can address our national needs and our international moral obligations. Labour's policies must change with the changing world but our values like our vision can still be fixed on that better world to come. Nothing less would be worthy of our past. Nothing less can open up the enormous potential of the future.

Peter Watt

Building a Party for the Future

Peter was the General Secretary of the Labour Party from 2005 – 2007 before resigning in the wake of the so called 'Donorgate' scandal. In January 2010 Peter published a hard-hitting account of his time as General Secretary, 'Inside Out'. The book was a highly personal account of the inner workings of the top of the Labour Party through some of its most turbulent times.

I remember my first conference speech as General Secretary. I told a story that I hoped would be funny, always a risk I know. It actually went down quite well and went something like this:

> *Many of you will have made friends, good friends in the party. So have I, in fact it is thanks to the party that I met my wife.*
>
> *I remember the first time that we met. I was a local organiser in Battersea – my first job with the party having left nursing. I arrived at the party office one day to check up on how the stuffing of our latest direct-mail was going. There were about fifteen people in the room all beavering away. Across the room I spotted a new face*

– and it took my breath away. This new volunteer was stuffing envelopes faster than anyone else in the room. Those of you who have organised such activity will know how I felt – someone who could stuff envelopes that fast was pure gold – I was hooked, it was love at first sight. I went over to introduce myself.

'Hello, I'm Peter Watt the local organiser' – I said. I could tell that she was impressed.She introduced herself as Vilma, and I sat next to her to help with the direct-mail. After a pleasant half an hour or so I decided to make my move. 'What are you doing tonight?' I asked, 'Do you fancy a drink?' To my surprise she said 'yes' and, eager not to lose the moment, I said 'great, there is a group of us meeting at 6 to go canvassing, see you there – we always go for a drink when we have finished'.

Conference – Vilma turned up at 6. Several months went by and we became 'good friends'. But Conference, I wanted more, I wanted commitment. One evening I decided that the time had come. I chose the moment to ask carefully. We were alone – it was after all an intimate moment and, mouth dry, I asked her, 'Vilma, will you do me the honour', she looked at me, I continued, 'the honour of accompanying me to the CLP AGM'.

Now, it wasn't a very funny story although people laughed. But I am embarrassed to say that it is almost true. I suspect that the reason it went down well was that the delegates recognised the sentiment. It spoke of a Party that was part cult, part social club and part (if we're honest) weird. The reason for joining may have been to change the world, but the reality was meetings, envelope-stuffing and leaflets. Back then Party membership was a closed and rarefied world with its own language, social calendar and values system – and it hasn't much changed since then.

The problem is that political parties in their current form are in trouble. The membership of political parties in the UK is declining and has been doing so since the 1960s.[2] Currently the numbers of those choosing to be members of political parties is hovering at around 1% of the electorate down from 4% as recently as 1983. Being a member of a political party is a minority sport. In terms of participation it is more handball than football. The problem is that within that minority an even smaller minority of activists form the small pool that gets elected, chooses candidates, decides policy and makes decisions on behalf of everyone else.

The very nature of political parties means that all too often party activists are divorced from the lives of those whose lives that they seek to influence. Activists mostly socialise together, mostly discuss issues only with each other, mostly read the same newspapers and blogs. They have their own language, culture and social norms (social norms that often other non-members find distinctly abnormal). We then use 'member engagement' as a proxy for finding out what the electorate think and feel and spend huge amounts of resources feeding the insatiable appetite that is the party bureaucracy at every level of our organisation.

We also do have an unfortunate habit on the left of sounding pious which doesn't help! I wrote about this habit in a posting for Labour Uncut in December 2010:

> *But there is arrogance at the heart of our politics that is going to make it difficult to really understand why we lost. It is an arrogance that says that we alone own morality and that we alone want the best for people. It says that our instincts and our motives alone are pure. It's an arrogance that belittles others' fears and concerns as "isms" whilst raising ours as righteous. We then mistakenly define ourselves as being distinctive from our opponents because we are morally superior rather than*

because we have different diagnoses and solutions. It is lazy, wrong and politically dangerous.[3]

Throw in an unhealthy mix of MPs expense scandals. Add a regular dose of day-day petty political squabbling, the sort of thing that we all love and that the electorate hates – is it any wonder that huge swathes of the electorate look at politics, politicians and political parties with disdain? When they complain that *'they're only in it for themselves'*, *'they don't know what it's like'*, or *'they're not the same as us'*, don't they all too often have a point? Trust in politics has never been high and the trend is for lower levels of trust.[4] Meanwhile, voters are less and less tribal in their affiliations. Yet within the body politic we still value political activism, (tribalism) as the highest and best form of involvement in politics. Our candidates have to impress fellow activists rather than voters in order to get selected. Our internal institutions feel cliquey and, despite all of the evidence to the contrary, we still talk of building a mass membership party.

I am certainly not knocking Party activism and certainly not activists. On the contrary, I am one! It is activists that deliver leaflets, phone voters and yes, stuff envelopes. It is activists that trudge the streets during by-elections and buy tickets to fundraising dinners. Without them there would be no Party and no local campaigns. Without them there would be no conferences, no audiences for set piece speeches and of course no candidates. But is that all that we are? All that we offer to potential members?

If we are to do more than manage the steady decline of our party organisation, then we must acknowledge that this is a political as well as an organisational problem. We need to rebuild a party that both celebrates traditional activism but also recognises its limitations. We must use the opportunity that we currently have to reform ourselves. Not just a few tweaks but fundamental reform so that our party is fit for purpose.

How can this be achieved?

Whatever we do we will still need to fundraise, leaflet, canvass and stuff those envelopes. Whatever we do we still have to make sure that our members are valued and celebrated. And whatever we do we will still need an organisational structure at local, regional and national level. Of course we still need to choose candidates and leaders. But we also need to regain a sense of legitimacy with much of the electorate with our focus being as much on voters as on our own internal structures. There probably isn't a perfect solution but here is my twelve point plan that I think will go some way to refocusing our organisation:

1. Firstly, I don't think that we should tinker too much with local party structures. They work on the whole and the process of changing them would be more trouble than it's worth. As Luke Akehurst blogged in November 2010[5], if you were designing a political party from scratch then you probably wouldn't design it like the Labour Party:

   But you probably would design from scratch an organisational structure that involved party units covering the levels of election the party fights: branch parties to fight ward elections and select and hold councillors to account, CLPs to fight parliamentary elections and select and hold MPs and PPCs to account, LGCs to co-ordinate council selections, elections and manifestos. i.e. broadly the structure we've got. You might want to encourage those party units to organise more socials and more campaigning and a few fewer meetings but the basic skeleton of the party makes sense and where populated with a reasonable number of people of good will, it works (we did win a hat-trick of general elections not that long ago).

So there is no overwhelming reason to change and our members are familiar with the current structures.

2. We should stop trying to systematically build a mass membership party. It wastes resources, focus and effort and is almost certainly fruitless. I don't mean stop recruiting; we should always ask supporters to join. Members should have the tools to recruit and asking should form a part of all election scripts. But those who want to join will generally do so anyway – most members now join online in any case.

3. Choosing Parliamentary candidates should be by primaries of all voters in the constituency with the shortlist being drawn up by local party members. All voters would be invited to attend the primaries with no bar apart from the need to register their details in advance.

    Some people worry that this would lead to local political opponents deliberately hijacking the process and somehow choosing the least able candidate. However there is no evidence that this happened when the Conservatives used primaries to choose some of their candidates for the 2010 general election. And of course the fact that local party members choose the shortlist should mitigate this.

    What it would do is make the local party and potential candidates focus on the electorate. The characteristics of shortlisted candidates would need to be those valued by the electorate, not necessarily those that are just valued by activists. It would give an internal party process an external focus whilst preserving the rights of members.

4. Local Government candidates should still be chosen by local party members – organising primaries at such a local level may be too organisationally onerous. However, if a local party wants to use primaries then it should be allowed to do so.

5. The public must be involved in party leadership elections. Currently the elections are in the form of an electoral college that represents the major internal party stakeholders. A third of votes goes to each of the MPs & MEPs, members and affiliated members.* The electoral college should become a four way college with the addition of the public. Each section should have 25% of the votes. Anyone should be allowed to vote in the public section as long as they register online first.

6. In the same way that the public should be involved in leadership elections they should also be involved in elections for the leaders in Wales and Scotland and for directly elected Mayoral candidates.

7. We were formed in part by trade unions, who wanted to see working class representation in Parliament. Constitutionally we recognise individual and collective memberships and as such the affiliated trade unions are members of our party in their own right. The right of affiliated members to act collectively is a fundamental part of our constitution. But the way that the relationship works at the moment is a sham. Far from being a relationship with millions of working people it is a relationship with a small group of trade union elites.

So in the future, individual affiliated members should be just that. They should individually have a direct relationship with the party in addition to their collective membership through their trade union. Affiliates should be required to ask their individual affiliated members permission to pass their details to the Labour Party. This would both confirm the individual's desire to actually be members (through their union) and also allow the party to contact them directly. Would this reduce the number of affiliated members? Yes, but it is a more honest reflection of the reality of the relationship and is certainly more politically defensible than the status-quo.

It will also require affiliated trade unions themselves to explain the benefits of affiliation directly to individual members and not just their activists who vote at their conferences. It would begin the process of turning the affiliated relationship into a relationship that genuinely reaches beyond the tiny number of senior trade unionists that currently run the 'politics' of affiliates.

8. The size of the voting blocs at the annual conference should be changed so that affiliates have 40% (as opposed to 50% currently) and constituency parties have 60% (as opposed to 50% currently). This still reflects the importance of our affiliates but puts the balance firmly in favour of individual members who are being represented at conference by their local party.

9. Currently any member, any part of the party, can submit resolutions to the party's policy making process. The reality of the current system is that small groups of individuals, often with vested interests, who understand the complexities of the 'rolling policy making process' can exert greater influence. That may be understandable but it is certainly not sustainable because the key vested interest that is missing is the electorate.

Submissions should therefore be required to be accompanied by evidence that voters, those affected by the proposal, and members, have all been involved in its development. This will institutionalize listening to the views of voters as well as activists and will become a part of an ongoing relationship-building process – a key part of sustained electoral success.

Local party units would need to link up with local voluntary groups, service users, trade unions and voters generally in order to evidence the veracity of their submission. It would forge links with individuals and groups beyond the local party elite and would help the party locally to become a friend and supporter of other forms of local activism.

The party should invest in the skills that members use to engage with voters when they are eliciting their views and attitudes on policy matters. There are more (and better) ways than just voter ID and direct-mail to engage with people. Local members could be trained to carry out their own focus groups, paired interviews and surveys, and to review existing data available locally. It could be a hugely liberating and informative process as members' skills and the quality of policy discussion improves.

10. The party should continue to deliver online tools that support members. The *Membersnet* approach has been hugely beneficial with initiatives like the online phonebank opening up campaigns to more and more members. But there is still an (understandable) culture of command and control within the party. At the same time the online world has opened up, as has the flow of information and the ability of people to network. Quite frankly the party has failed to keep pace. In future the party should, in addition to delivering bespoke tools like the online phonebank, simply encourage members, supporters (even occasional supporters) to network and collaborate using existing online tools. The opportunities afforded by the rapidly changing communications and social media market cannot be controlled and the party will not like everything that emerges. But on balance the benefits of networking and collaborating will hugely outweigh any negatives.

11. The party should accept that the detail of policy cannot be written by a committee let alone an entire party membership. In the end every manifesto is written by someone trusted by the leader. This has to be a good thing – it is the leader, after

all, who has to front up the policy platform. We should drop the pretence that our manifestos are developed by our members – it just leads to heartache and let down all ways round.

Our leaders must, though, be prepared to seriously listen to members, to their submissions, to the public and to their colleagues. But ultimately the leader needs to decide on the manifesto and be prepared to defend it within the party and critically with the public. Does this devalue submissions from the party? On the contrary, the current pretence that the party makes policy (rather than the leader) devalues the submissions. Better to be honest so that all sides know where they stand.

12. Finally the manifesto (or its precursor) should undergo an approval process that involves the party and the voters. In 1996 we had the 'Road to the Manifesto' process that successfully engaged the party. In future we should repeat this but include voters. It won't be perfect but it will be better than not trying to involve people.

There is almost nothing that gets party members' pulses racing as much as plans to change party rules and organisation. The framework and familiarity are comfortable and understandably we generally don't like change. But the truth is that, along with other parties, our current organisation is in decline. If we are to halt and then reverse this trend then we need to take action now. Simply tweaking will show that we haven't fully understood the serious organisational and consequential political hole that we are in. There isn't much about opposition that is good. But one thing that it allows is a time for reform of our organisation.

We shouldn't waste the opportunity.

The Rt Hon Lord Temple-Morris

Progressive Politics

Lord Temple-Morris was the MP for Leominster between 1974 and 2001. He was Chair of Cambridge University Conservatives Association in 1961 and was called to the Bar in 1962. He was a practising Barrister who became a Solicitor in 1989 and remains today a practising Consultant Solicitor and Labour Peer. He defected to Labour from the Conservatives in 1998.

Now is the time to seize the moment whilst in opposition and get it right. On the one hand the Coalition has given us a clear field of fire on the centre left. If we take the opportunity there is a real prospect that we can become the UK's most powerful political party, the natural representative of the majority, and the natural party of government. On the other hand failure to modernise and equip ourselves for this task means an uncertain future as an opposition party and, on occasion, in government if we are lucky.

For me modernisation means taking full credit for our distinguished past but also using and adapting it to become the party of all the people and in all parts of the country. I say this coming from a Tory background; my father was a Tory MP and I served 23 years on the Conservative benches before taking the difficult decision to leave my party and cross the floor to Labour. My decision to become Labour was a very public choice and I have no regrets. Fighting ten general elections against Labour and the Liberals gives me a certain perspective and certainly qualification to comment.

My politics have never changed. I could be summed up as a 'One Nation Conservative with a social conscience' or equally as a social democratic member of the Labour Party. When I went up to Cambridge in 1958, the choice of political party for myself and many others was virtually automatic. We became Conservative because of background and aspiration. We all fancied ourselves on the left of the Tory Party which was all there was for us. There was no social democratic option available as we saw it and the Liberals were not a practical proposition. Looking back I would have been much happier on the centre left of politics from the outset but, for better or worse, I did not see Labour as a political home. The purpose of this piece is to help make Labour an attractive option for all; of whatever class, background, colour or creed.

The history and origin of the Labour Party is important, in that it came into being in the cause of an historically necessary class struggle. It became a movement to this end and made the major contribution towards the creation of a more balanced and civilised society. Part of our problem today is that the legacy of our distinguished history is still with us. It has left us short of being a national party in the complete sense of the word. We may be the party of the north; of Wales and Scotland; of the inner cities and the deprived; but we are not the natural party of the more prosperous and populated centre and south of England. This situation, so well identified by Giles Radice in his "Southern Discomfort" series, is at the very heart of Labour's problems for the future. Their solution provides the key to all of this.

To say that Labour has, on occasion, won the centre and south of England is the exception proving the rule. 1945 was the post-war cry for a new society and the Attlee Government did not let the country down. 1964 was a time of Tory decline, a mood for change and Labour's ability to present the right leader at the right time to the people. Harold Wilson in 1964 was at the height of his powers and represented the change that people wanted. This combination of mood and leadership quite overcame any historical baggage that Labour might have been potentially carrying in the centre and south of England. Similarly, in 1997 there was a seriously diminished and divided Tory Party contrasted with a quite outstanding Labour leader in Tony Blair. With or without the Iraq issue he remained the dominant force in British politics for ten years and delivered the centre and south sufficiently for three consecutive election victories. This we should learn from and be proud of.

The main lesson is to build on what we have done and consider what we are. Looking at it from the outside, the Labour Party does not quite seem to get enough credit for its considerable accomplishments. The foundation of our modern state occurred in the 1945-51 period yet seems taken for granted; the 1960s was a vital decade of social change certainly made easier by a centre-left government. The achievements of the Blair period, constitutionally, electorally and socially are to be lauded and never denied; similarly the social spending of Gordon Brown, together with his international financial management at a time of need – all of which represent considerable Labour Governmental achievements. That is progress to be proud of and to be built upon. No blank sheets but rather a turning of the page.

So where do we start? To my mind it has to be with the party itself. A party of all the people, astride the political middle ground but tilting it to the centre left. A modern party, both nationally and internationally, dedicated to fairness and equality of opportunity. But, as we have recently proved, capable of good financial management which is essential to producing the wealth necessary to achieve social change and improvement. We have achieved much of this but more is needed.

My basic remedies may or may not be practical politics but they need to be discussed, as they have been in the past, but more than ever now. For me they are in the same bracket as Clause 4 and OMOV, both of which problems for Labour have been faced up to. In whole or in part, in recent years, the first basic question is our name itself. The name "Labour" brings together the strands of the Labour Movement. A combination of individuals, trade unions, other movements and intellectuals that was dedicated to representing and bettering the situation of the working classes. A necessary and worthy cause that, in the historical context, we have largely fulfilled, given that we must always continue to represent the less fortunate within the political system. However our name comes from our past and doesn't best promote the cause of those who, as a whole, we need to represent in the future.

The country has steadily become more and more middle class. This very much applies in the centre and south of England. Perspectives change with circumstances as people have steadily left the heavy industrial and public sectors and emerged as white-collar or skilled workers. They tend to associate Labour with their or their parents' past. Their aspirations for the future make them liable to look elsewhere politically and we can't always rely on brilliant leaders to get us over this reality.

I come back to the name. Any change in this area will encounter resistance and the matter is complicated by the perambulations of the name 'Social Democrat' over recent years. That said I submit that those considering these matters should look at the possibility of the description 'Social Democratic and Labour Party of the United Kingdom'. This gains much and sacrifices little. It should also add the Northern Ireland SDLP to us as a worthy sister party which they are de facto in any event.

There is an added attraction here in that we could be entering a period where coalition governments are increasingly on the cards.

This name would be much more attractive to the middle ground generally and to the disillusioned Liberal Democrat voter in particular. In addition there is a natural middle class inclination to like to think of itself as 'social democrat'. This was very evident when the SDP was formed in 1982 but a mood was not enough for a new party. It could however be of enormous advantage to us.

The next question is the continuation of this process in creating a *modern party structure*. This means the translation of the Labour Movement into a modern equivalent. The key here is to build upon and not to destroy the elements of the Labour Movement, and in particular the role of the trade unions is historic, vital and constructive. This must continue but not in a way that prevents us from becoming a modern 'one member one vote' party. It should not be beyond the wit of our review to find ways whereby the unions can work alongside us, perhaps by being affiliated in some way, but not wielding any sort of elective power. This would obviously not include the thousands of union members who would hopefully become full party members and vote in the same way as everyone else. I have no hesitation in saying that this change would do more good in those areas of the country where we have electoral difficulties than anything else. If we had the name as well we really would be going places.

Part of this reform is the way the leader of our party is elected. It should follow naturally that a 'one member one vote' party can do without the extra votes given to affiliated bodies and the unions. The third Electoral College should disappear. A proper balance of power can then be worked out between the Parliamentary Party and the party in the country. The constitution and membership of the National Executive Committee; the powers of conference; any role for a Chairman of the Labour Party; our overall constitution and anything else also relevant will also have to be reviewed as part of this. The outcome will hopefully be a modern and very electable Social Democratic and Labour Party.

The other half of the overall equation is policy. A modern party needs modern policies consistent with its beliefs. It is not my intent here to go into policy detail but merely add some general thoughts. Above all people need to know where we are going and what we stand for. To begin with we should not hesitate to stand for what we have always stood for and are known to stand for; a fair and just society which cares for the weak and gives an equal chance for all to shine. Dogma from wherever has to be out. Change consistent with our beliefs has to be encouraged and not least in the fields of health and education. Commerce and finance must be free to operate but do so responsibly. Very important here is for us to be European and internationalist in outlook so that we may be big enough to make a difference and not least in controlling the excesses of commerce, industry and banking.

The European Union has a vital role in all this as does our overall international role and good name in promoting the vital causes of climate change and international development. Much of this is very natural political territory for us, which it is certainly not for today's Conservative party.

I end where I began. Now is the time and we must seize the opportunity. By the next election we must be firmly and attractively in the centre but coming from the centre-left. We have to be ready to take on all-comers and not just win by default. There is a joker in the pack in that we could face some sort of pact or electoral arrangement between the coalition parties. A modern Social Democratic and Labour Party could beat the lot of them, together or apart. Let us do that!

Tracey J Cheetham

Social Media and Labour

Tracey has established a major social media presence over the last few years, with a well-respected blog at www.tchee.co.uk. She has a reputation for fairness and an eye for well researched detail. She is, among her other activities, in the writing-up phase of her PhD, a qualified teacher, Constituency Manager for a busy MP and a mum of three. She is also a digital ambassador for Save the Children, having recently visited Mozambique on their behalf for a campaign which garnered around 30 million hits online. Tracey is also proud to be a Labour Councillor on Barnsley MBC.

M ost organisations are realising the impact that social media can have on their public relations and brand identity. Large corporations have routine keyword alerts, with employees who are paid to watch what is being said about the company online. This may sound a little like control-freakery and more than slightly paranoid, but the foundation is based on one of the fundamental issues in customer service. If you or I go into a store or telephone company and receive excellent service, we may smile about it ... if we notice. We may mention it to one or two people ... if we remember. However, if you or I go into a store or call a company and are dissatisfied with the service we receive, we will tell everyone we know. In the days before social media, when we might talk about it at work, to family and to a few friends at the school gate/pub/gym, the impact was small. Now, we tell thousands of people, with one click of a mouse. This is why everyone, from the biggest corporations to the smallest local SMEs, are tapping into the marketplace that is being created in this virtual world of chatter.

The use of social media (SocMed) is not just a private sector phenomenon, the public and voluntary sectors are also established in the virtual SocMed environment. Charities now have Social Media Officers and online campaigns can reach thousands or even millions of people in a very short period of time. An excellent example of this is the #PassItOn campaign, which was used by Save the Children to try to influence international governments. It reached almost unbelievable **30 million people**, in just a few weeks.

Given statistics like that, it is easy to overestimate the impact of social media. The difference is in the type of activity it is used for *and* in strategic, specific use. Of the various forms that social media takes, the most popular/far-reaching are Twitter and Facebook, with Twitter having the advantage of wider distributive potential due to users being able to 'tag' posts.

On Twitter, trending topics are a sign of widescale distribution. These are the keywords or phrases that are being tweeted above all others. Tweeps (the common name for people who use Twitter) have three main aims: increasing their follower count, getting their tweets RT'd or 'Retweeted' and starting a trending topic. On Facebook, it is all about how many friends, fans or 'likes' and on blogs, it is about checking the weekly page view statistics. Put these into perspective and one can see clearly, they are all about one thing: popularity.

Savvy organisations know that to get RTs and spread the

message about their latest product, they must provide an incentive. Major supermarkets have generated huge numbers of RTs by using them as the means of entering a competition; "RT to be in with a chance of winning a new flipcam/iPad/box of chocolates!" It is very easy to enter a draw or competition, if you can do so with just one or two clicks of the mouse.

This leads us on to activism. Consider how many campaigns in recent years have included an online petition. Don't get me wrong, many people sign online petitions and back that up with action. There are, however some people who do care and would like to do something, if they could tear themselves away from their PC/Macbook/iPad or smartphone. Social media gives them the ability to do that, in fact, it provides the perfect platform for, what we can term 'lazy activists'. Sign a petition in support of healthy eating in schools? – *CLICK!* Object to live animal exports? – *CLICK!* Against the government's cuts? – *CLICK!* In favour of the government's cuts? – *CLICK!*

For every [online] action, there is an equal and opposite [online] reaction. With all this easy, online engagement, it is obvious why political parties all use social media as a way of spreading their message. The key is in clever, specific and tactical use of the various channels available.

Politics and social media are excellent bedfellows. Trending topics on Twitter frequently reflect the current big news stories or television programme being watched along with thousands of other audience members who watch and Tweet, using the agreed hashtag. Some good examples of this are #bbcqt (Question Time), #hignfy (Have I Got News For You) and one-off events always feature a hashtag, such as the leaders' debates ahead of the General Election 2010. Political activists of all parties watched them and engaged in their own debates via Twitter. It was largely partisan stuff, with the Conservative Tweeps declaring Cameron was the winner, the Liberal Democrat Tweeps saying it was Clegg who nailed it and the Labour Party Tweeps insisting it was Brown. No surprises there then, but what effect, if any, did this have on engagement?

The Labour Party was at the forefront of embracing and using social media as a means of spreading the message and engaging members. Perspective is key and analysts must take a holistic approach to gauge support, it is easy to overestimate the value of online activity and as a result, get your offline activity wrong.

This was one area, evident during the 2010 General Election campaign, when the voice of online activists, being so loud, dominated several mainstream or 'offline' events. There were many occasions where Gordon Brown or a senior minister would be surrounded by Labour students and party Twitterati. Many party members, of an older generation, some online, some not, commented on how this did not reflect the party membership. It did though, if you look only at the online demographic; it is weighted, as one might expect, towards members who are younger and/or students and easily rounded up through online networking.

If you mainly interacted with the large, online Labour community, it would have been easy to assume that the election was going to be a walk in the park and a fourth term was inevitable. John Prescott ran his 'Go Fourth' campaign and successfully merged online and offline activity; using Twitter to arrange Tweet-ups, that were a mix of both types of activists.

Mobilisation of already-engaged activists is one of the main strengths of online campaigning. Social media is an excellent tool for reaching and motivating those who are already on board with your message. This was proven during a local council by-election in St Helen's ward, Barnsley, where activists heard about it via SocMed and travelled cross-country to help the thinly-stretched local team. This led in turn to a huge Labour presence on the streets and a resounding win.

The key lesson is to combine those members reached through online activity, with those who are not in this virtual set. Each will be a good influence on the other. The key lesson is that no party can have one form of activity, without the other. No matter how much online activity is going on, no matter how many blogs and Twitter-supporters/Facebook fans you have; nothing beats getting out on the doorstep and transferring all that support into actual, physical campaigning.

Once elected to local or national government, members can, and many do, engage with their communities and constituents via social media. Cllr Tim Cheetham of Barnsley MBC gives the best description of why this is important, when answering the cynics and critics of this type of engagement. He says, "If you were in your ward or constituency and noticed a gathering of twenty, thirty or two-hundred people, you would want to join in, to hear what they were saying, and find out what the local issues are. You would not walk on by and ignore it. If you do not engage with social media, that is exactly what you are doing; walking past one of the places where many of the people you represent are gathering, and talking about local issues, every single day".

The Labour Party seems to understand this ideology and has embraced online campaigning and activism; leading to the emergence of several big-hitters in the virtual world of politics. Labour MP Kerry McCarthy, was given a portfolio that included online engagement and the use of new media. Along with Kerry, Tom Harris MP and Tom Watson MP were among the first Members of Parliament to have a significant online identity and who actually engaged with other SocMed users. It isn't only MPs though, it is almost impossible, once elected to public office, to *not* have an online presence. Local Councils, Parliament and many local party branches will have pages dedicated to those who are representing the people and the party. Many local councillors and members of parliament have a Facebook page and/or a Twitter feed. Those that do this most successfully, are the ones who actually interact with their followers.

Social media should never be simply a broadcast service. If you want to do that, send out a press release or take out a poster site. The whole point of SocMed is *engagement*. There are Twitter accounts that are following absolutely no-one. Talk about only liking the sound of your own voice! Following only their close personal friends and a few colleagues, does not bode well for the opportunity (or concern) of MPs to hear what the public or their constituents are saying.

In the run up to the General Election 2010, Twitter was abuzz with politics. Now clearly, the result was not the outcome Labour wanted, however, had you been part of the Labour Twitterati, you would have been confident, no, convinced, that the election was in the bag for Labour. This is where a good dose of 'reality-check' comes in. SocMed must always be a side dish to the main course of 'IRL' (in real life, for the non-nerds amongst you) activity.

It is here that perspective is key. Many people on Twitter, follow only those they agree with. There are several Labour activists who absolutely, will not follow Tory Tweeps; one I know of, calls it a personal Twitter policy. This is where the limitation of SocMed is most apparent. How can anyone have the full picture if they only listen to people they agree with? This applies whether it is broad or narrow differences, there are undoubtedly Labour Tweeps who do not follow other Labour Tweeps, because they disagree on certain issues; as always, we are a broad church – even online.

In the lead up to what was tagged on Twitter as #GE10, Twitter was an excellent debating ground. If you managed to avoid the trolls, (of which there are many) who are merely looking to begin a flame war, (for those of you who are not in tune with the lingo here, it is the online equivalent of Richard Littlejohn) it was a great way of really understanding the grassroots opinions of opposition parties.

The mainstream media was mostly batting against Labour, yet online, there were many voices speaking for us. The blogosphere was beginning to shift from the dominance of the right-wing commentators such as Iain Dale and Guido Fawkes. Although they were still prominent, the emergence of Political Scrapbook, Left Foot Forward and LabourList, started to redress the balance. The combination of blogging and SocMed, expands the audience incredibly. This is where the popularity contest really pays off, as the more RTs and cross-posting on Facebook; the more visitors will click onto the blog.

The Labour Blogosphere has exploded, particularly since we became the opposition party. It is always easier to write about what the government is getting wrong, than to write something saying "aren't we great!" without being sycophantic. It is true to say that some (on all sides) see their blog as a way to help them into Westminster. One only has to read the sycophantic ramblings of some would-be-PPCs to know this is true.

There are those who are cynical about the use of social media and it is true to say that not everyone who has used it, has had a positive experience. The first thing people do, whether in receipt of a job application, seeing a name in the paper, or trying to see what former classmates are doing, is to employ their Google-Fu. Google brings everything, good and bad, to the fore. This is great, if you have never made a mistake or said anything, in jest, that can later be used against you in a selection interview. Social media not only highlights the activism and good work done for the party, but it is also like the worst kind of eternal-elephant. It never forgets.

The mainstream media is feeling the effects of the social media phenomenon and competition for jobs in journalism is at an all time high. Print media just cannot keep up with the fastest spreading news system around. Twitter is frequently the place where news breaks. Perhaps this is why the print media has in the past turned its wrath on Twitter and those who use it.

A civil servant, whose Twitter feed was absolutely nothing to do with her job, tweeted about her social life. One national newspaper made a story of this, as though, because this tweep was a civil servant, she should not go out, or drink, or have a life. There has also been more than one career-death, purely because of an ill-judged tweet that subsequently ended up in the mainstream media. SocMed is a means of exposure, often to an unforgiving audience and as well as being the source of lazy activism, it is also the domain of lazy journalism.

Of course, not all Tweeps were innocent, sending intimate photographs via Twitter or similar SocMed app, is never going to be a good career move and this practice has also seen some high-profile scalps in recent years. This is where mainstream and new media crossover is at its worst, do something dodgy online, it will cross over to mainstream; get into the local newspaper for having a scrap down the pub, it will cross over to online. Either way, the audience, thanks to online activity, will be multiplied.

The best/worst example of this is the Robin Hood Airport incident, where a frustrated traveller ended up with a criminal record because of a tweet in jest, saying he would blow the airport up. Probably not the wisest thing to joke about, but nonetheless, just a flippant remark from someone who then felt the full force of the justice system.

The negatives aside, most of which come down to common sense, there are enormous benefits to social media and online activity. The Labour Party is truly an online player and mostly does it well. As for the ultimate question of whether SocMed can influence the outcome of an election? No. Not yet, while undoubtedly there is potential for influence on a small scale, election results are still influenced mostly by mainstream, broadcast media, where the message can be controlled and no one can answer back.

The Future for British Defence, Justice, Law & Order

Admiral the Rt Hon Lord West of Spithead, GCB, DCS

Defence: The Most Important Duty of Government, but Sadly not a Vote Winner?

Admiral Lord West has served as Chief of Defence Intelligence, First Sea Lord, and, for 3 years, Minister for Security, Counter Terrorism and Cyber Security at the Home Office.

In 1998, the Labour Government produced a Strategic Defence Review to almost universal acclaim. It had taken the best part of two years to complete and, for the first time since World War II, was conducted in conjunction with the Foreign Office and its policy objectives. Some twelve years later the Coalition Government produced its Strategic Defence and Security Review (SDSR) to almost universal condemnation after some five months in power. In theory it was driven by the requirements of the National Security Strategy (NSS) but that link was somewhat tenuous. Indeed the lack of coherence of some of the decisions – paying off the newly refitted HMS Ark Royal and scrapping our best, indeed only real close support aircraft, the Harrier – has left military experts, academics and allies dumbfounded and our rivals and possible enemies, contemptuous. Bizarrely, there were other options that would have achieved greater savings with less strategic risk.

There is no doubt that the UK's situation in 1998 was very different from that in 2010. Unlike today, the country was not grappling with the aftermath of a global financial crisis and severe recession. However, some myths do need to be put to bed. If one looked at the Ministry of Defence's long-term programmes and commitments in 1998 and used the same methodology as Liam Fox for his £36Bn 'black hole', there would have been a black hole of some £28Bn.

When Labour took over power from the Conservatives in 1997 the ill-judged and badly run Typhoon programme was out of control. At the same time, despite constant warnings from the naval staff, the delay (until 1996) in ordering the Astute class submarines had almost destroyed our in-house capability to design and construct such complex platforms and meant there would inevitably be an uncontrollable growth in cost. Having cancelled the disastrous Nimrod AEW programme in the late 1980s, the Conservatives embarked on the equally ill-fated Nimrod MRA4 programme in December 1996. The Complex alliance politics and disagreements over requirements had for twelve years bedevilled the multi-national programme (NFR90/CNGF) for a warship with which we hoped to replace the Type 42 destroyers. This was inevitably leading to a delayed and more expensive replacement, which became the Type 45 programme. The disgraceful purchase of 8 SF Chinooks without appropriate software support had been made in 1995 and the illogical ownership of the support helicopter force by the RAF rather than the Army was already impacting on sensible decisions regarding its procurement needs.

So having conducted a good Defence Review how was Labour's stewardship of defence? Problems arose almost immediately as it became apparent that the clearly articulated and welcomed programme was not being fully funded. Indeed from year one there was an £800 million annual shortfall. It was extremely unfortunate that Defence (MOD) could not get its voice heard

above that of other departments but military power was not considered a vote winner. Indeed whether intended or not, Labour gave the impression as the administration ran on, that the post of Secretary of Defence was not one of the most important cabinet positions. Perceptions, however erroneous, are hard to dislodge. For instance, there is a general view that the Conservatives are more willing to invest in Defence than Labour, which since 1930 is far from the case. The gap in funding from 1998 was particularly unfortunate as national wealth burgeoned and money could have been found with little pain by siphoning off a small proportion of the National Health Service's massive increase in resources or those devoted to giving DFID too much money before it was able to use it wisely or well.

The other factor was that the Prime Minister was using the military more and more: Operation Desert Fox against Iraq in 1998, the Kosovo conflict in early 1999, East Timor in late 1999, Sierra Leone in early 2000, the invasion of Afghanistan late 2001 and the invasion of Iraq in early 2003. It is regrettable that the Prime Minister as First Lord of the Treasury failed to ensure that the Chancellor fully funded Defence. Although the costs of those operations were meant to be found from the reserve, they never quite were. Consequently, the impact of a steady underfunding and greater military involvement was having a pernicious effect.

The Conservatives had left procurement in a mess and although Lord Drayson made huge strides in that area, not least in the early work on the Defence Industrial Strategy, there remained considerable unfinished business. The worst programmes were primarily those initiated in the early and mid 1990s.

Several factors had a huge impact on the Labour Government's popularity and its defence credentials such as the controversial invasion of Iraq and the mishandling of its aftermath; the flawed decision to remain in Afghanistan after the initial invasion post 9/11 and the equally flawed decision to move into the Helmand region with its consequent toll on our servicemen's lives.

In addition the impression, albeit incorrect, that our military were going into harm's way without adequate funding became a recurrent theme on the floor of the House. There is no doubt that the underfunding of the core defence budget from 1998 onwards, was the reason for that perception even though total defence spending was growing. The reality is that by 2008/9 our people had never before been so well equipped for an operation in which they were involved. And in Harrier GR9 we deployed what our people in harm's way knew and said was the best close support aeroplane in the alliance in Afghanistan, apart from possibly the A-10 Warthog of the USAF.

The 1998 review clearly identified the need for the UK to be a global player, capable of expeditionary operations and one key difference from the preceding years was the realisation that to conduct such operations required two large aircraft carriers. The two new large strike carriers were the centrepiece of the 1998 Defence Review, and all policy work throughout the first decade of the millennium showed that they were needed. That requirement was supported by the latest Coalition NSS and SDSR 2010 but the carrier programme illustrated some of the inherent problems within defence procurement. First, the initial cost estimate was quite clearly too low (the triumph of optimism) and there was a steady struggle over the first years of the millennium to provide a realistic funding line. As First Sea Lord, I was effectively forced to give up excellent frigates that we sorely needed as I was made to find the money for the carriers from within the "maritime programme". It was a mistake and I should have fought harder and asked to see the Prime Minister to obtain extra funding from the Treasury or from other less significant programmes within the Ministry of Defence. In addition there was entrenched opposition from areas of the civil service and military to their procurement. Some in Whitehall were opposed to the UK having the capability to intervene elsewhere in the world; without carriers, amphibious shipping and supporting naval assets our global reach would be curtailed – whether in the national interest or not.

Even though it was government policy to build the carriers, hurdles were constantly put in the programme's way, which led, for example, to the ridiculous slippage of the programme in 2008. Those same opponents hoped it would spell the end for the carriers in the 2010 Defence Review but, as it turned out, it just added £1.6Bn to their cost.

The 1998 review articulated the need to maintain our continuous at-sea nuclear deterrent but it was not until the early part of the new millennium that decisions had to be made about renewing the warheads and replacing the submarines. A funding line for the former was provided and the initial work to replace the submarine was embarked upon. It was agreed in principle that the capital costs of the replacement submarines would come from the reserve.

So what should Labour learn from its thirteen years in power and what is required for the future? The flawed SDSR in 2010 and significant reductions to our military, show that defence is not safe in the hands of the Coalition. The United States are worried about our ability to stand beside them and we are no longer the pre-eminent military power in Europe. It is interesting that Liam Fox in the 2007 Commons Defence debate described the existing defence force structure as woefully inadequate. It was of course significantly larger than that resulting from the SDSR over which Dr Fox has presided. David Cameron has been forced by his Coalition colleagues to kick the final decision on replacing our aging deterrent submarines outside of this parliament, making it a political football. At the same time he has forced the MOD to find the money from its already dramatically reduced budget rather than from the reserve.

The SDSR decision to go for the F35C aircraft for the carriers was correct but there is no clarity on whether or not both carriers will be fitted with catapults and arrester wires. If not, one can predict a scenario that when the nation needs to deploy a fully armed carrier, which it will, there will not be one in commission.

Post SDSR 2010, 2% of UK GDP is spent on defence – if money for current operations from the reserve is included – it is set to fall below this figure over the next four years to as low as 1.7% of GDP. As the reductions bite we will become a different nation. Can we really expect to remain a permanent member of the UN Security Council? How can we look after our dependencies? Perhaps we should ask France to take that responsibility? How can we justify running the majority of the world's shipping from London, with the International Maritime Organisation based there, when we are unable even to protect our own merchant fleet? Who will look after our five and a half million nationals and our vast investments overseas?

Our people and their commitment and courage are fundamental to the excellence of our military forces. They were seriously overstretched according to Liam Fox when in opposition and yet we are now running numbers down further. The Coalition has embarked on a new war whilst at the same time looking to reduce some of the personal allowances of our military personnel.

I am concerned that successive governments have been in some kind of denial. We are continuing to pretend that we can be a major international player and deploy military force without taking the trouble to invest in it now or in its future. Since we want something for which we are not prepared to pay the price, we should be prepared to make the strategic and policy choices which follow from this refusal. We are guilty of not giving the serious intellectual effort necessary to our position and strategic goals in the world, nor analysing the threats, risks and vulnerabilities that face us.

Labour must not make the same mistake in the future. Although to many it will not be a popular strategy, Labour should, I believe, make a clear commitment to increasing the percentage of GDP spent on defence to 2.5%. It is important to do what successive governments have not done which is face financial realities and align military ambitions and operations with budgets. However, the MOD does need fixing. For about £40 billion a year we are getting a pretty poor deal. Post SDSR 2010, we shall by 2015 have a Royal Navy which will be the smallest since Pepys' day, a Royal Air Force with less combat aircraft than Sweden, and an army which is one of the smallest amongst the top twenty or thirty nations and smaller than most major NATO countries' armies. We should ensure a root-and-branch change to MOD structures and how business is done.

Nothing should be off the agenda, even such controversial moves as rationalising down to two services – one responsible for continental warfare and one for maritime warfare. There should be more use made of a larger territorial army whilst reducing the number of regulars. The procurement process within the MOD, indeed more broadly across government, must be sorted out. The Bernard Gray report documented that chopping and changing by politicians wasted up to a third of the procurement budget. Let us tell the people frankly that we have learned our lesson for next time. We should show a clear commitment to supporting our high-tech defence industries in producing the best defence equipment in the world. We should be clear in our intention to build and run two carriers capable of operating the requisite maritime strike air group and continue to maintain our expeditionary capability.

Let us lead in rebuilding a cross-party consensus on the proper Defence of the Realm, following the example of the collaboration between Bob Ainsworth MP and Bernard Jenkin MP in their hard-hitting and important effort to force a public debate on just the issues I am raising here as well as a proper debate on the nature of our national interests.

Diplomacy, aid, the BBC world service, training of other nations' military, education of their youngsters, maximum leverage from the universality of English, use of bilateral and alliance relationships – these are many if not an exhaustive list of the things that can further the interests of our nation, enhance our wealth and, by fostering stability, help ensure our security. But this 'soft power' is weakened, if not powerless, if the aura of power that the possession of 'hard power' *and the will to use it*, confers.

There are real dangers of an extremely chaotic and highly dangerous world developing over the next decades, not least within the context of possibly irreversible climate change and ever increasing competition for resources of all kinds among a rapidly expanding world population. In the final analysis our national survival will depend as it always has on our military and, as an island nation, particularly on our maritime forces. Labour must show the lead where the Coalition has failed and keep our nation's sword and armour bright.

Trident?

Ashley Tiffen

A Socialist Law and Order Agenda

Ashley has over 30 years experience as a member of the police service including operational and training duties. After a spell in professional standards he worked in training in a British Overseas Territory before finally retiring. Since 2006, he has been a senior lecturer in Policing; his experiences leave him as a committed but pragmatic socialist.

Regardless of the issues of the day there are key areas of everyday life, the economy, education and law and order, which will always be part of the political debate. In honest moments socialists would have to acknowledge that in law and order the right wing agenda has resonated with the electorate. The questions today are: should the left continue to pursue policies that are widely rejected? Should policies be amended and, if so, will this be seen as a 'climb down' from socialist principles? Indeed, should the left abandon the law and order agenda entirely to the centre right, and meekly succumb to the right wing agenda?

The attempt, in the mid 1990s, to at least compete with a right wing agenda was, unfortunately, found to be no more than empty rhetoric. New Labour may have wanted to be seen to deal with the underlying issues of crime but to claim that a forthcoming administration was going to be 'tough on crime' was always going to be questioned.

Poverty, the failure of education for some groups and a poorly developed built environment, as notable examples, have led to feelings of worthlessness by some sections of society which, in turn, leads to criminality. These remain key areas where a socialist agenda can have a positive impact and where the claim to be 'tough on the causes of crime' can be justified, remembering, of course, that the electorate does not necessarily recognize these as law and order measures.

The key for the future is to develop law and order policies that clearly link to the wider socialist agenda of fairness but, at the same time, acknowledge the very real concerns of the public around their safety and protection. Policies that concede the rights that every man, woman and child have within our society, while also demanding that everyone has certain responsibilities to each other and to the society in which they live.

Importantly, in opposition, it is incumbent upon Labour to take the fight to the public by challenging the prevailing right agenda on crime. The Tory policies are simply empty rhetoric. Many of their current policies are clearly extensions of their monetarist policies designed to make the rich richer and keep the poor poor! One only has to look at how the policies of the current Coalition waver and change at the sign of any resistance. The plans of the Justice Minister, to all but eliminate short prison sentences in favour of community (and much more effective) punishments or to reduce sentences for an early guilty plea have their roots not in any law and order agenda but in the need to bend to the will of the Treasury. As soon as these plans were criticized as being 'soft on criminals' it was noticeable how the language hardened while the Treasury's agenda was quietly maintained.

We must challenge the Home Secretary who has suggested that the Police can cut costs by focusing on their core role of policing. This makes no sense: a fight to reduce crime and the harm it causes is not one just for the police or the courts or the prison and probation services, it is one where a holistic approach to deal with the very real problems of society has to sit alongside the need for specific actions to deal with specific events.

For example, dealing with the most prolific offenders requires a coordinated approach to their housing and employment needs alongside their mental health or drugs rehabilitation needs. It requires the police to work closely with, not only criminal justice partners, but with partners across the whole spectrum of society. To try and compartmentalize society, as Theresa May is suggesting, should be challenged at every opportunity.

The Conservatives do not have a monopoly on the law and order agenda by right. They have been handed it by a failure of the left to escape from the ideological challenges of advocating the rights of the individual over the responsibilities they have to society.

All too often the Labour agenda is perceived as developing and supporting individual rights while the right of centre agenda has focused on responsibilities, with Labour concentrating on, for example, human rights and the Conservatives seeing a capitalist social order articulated as the 'public good' as being primary. Now is the time to produce policies that balance the needs of the individual with the needs of an ordered and safe society.

The Right Realist criminology theory places the causes of crime firmly on the individual. It suggests that we all have a 'rational choice' whether or not to commit crime and that both hardening the potential target and developing increasingly deterring punishments can be effective in reducing crime. While it has to be acknowledged that this does appeal to the public one has to ask why does this have widespread appeal? If the theory is analysed there are key areas where it is flawed. Not everyone and certainly many of those who appear to have an inclination to commit crime have the ability to make a 'rational choice'.

It is widely recognized that many people who today finds themselves in prison are suffering from a diagnosable mental illness. Are they capable of making a 'rational choice'? Are all young offenders capable of adequately developing a cost–benefit analysis of their actions? How many crimes are committed 'on the spur of the moment' in a fit of rage or thoughtless frenzy? Do we dismiss the evidence that suggests society bears some responsibility because it is easier to have an individual in the dock? In these cases has society produced a class of people who happily claim their rights while ignoring their responsibilities? Or have we ignored the concept of social responsibility when dealing with perceived underclasses?

For example, society has a responsibility to provide a formal education system that develops the skills necessary to prosper in the adult world. Reading, writing and arithmetic or the 'Three R's' are, rightly, seen as the basic building blocks of education. But while young people have a right to this education, have we given less weight to the need for the responsibility they bear to engage with this opportunity? Is it not the responsibility of the parent to take a central role in the education process rather than abrogate this responsibility in favour of a right for their children 'to be educated'?

The widespread appeal of the Right Realist theories is predicated on the widespread belief that we are responsible parents. We all take a keen interest in our children and their development and education. We all teach them right from wrong. Unfortunately, this isn't always true. In the fast changing world in which we live today, how many people make the time to read to and with their children? How many parents trying to deal with an increasing workload while juggling some semblance of a family and social life abandon their children to CBeebies or an electronic game? Indeed, this is where the law and order debate becomes subsumed within the wider debate. Is it wrong to suggest that parents and children have responsibilities, either to be part of the teaching process or to be an active learner? Is it wrong to explain to a parent or carer that spending time regularly with a child looking at books has so many wonderful benefits both for the development of the child and their personal relationship?

This is where the debate on rights and responsibilities rests. All too often today we hear someone saying, "I have my rights" and rarely, "I have my responsibilities".

Of course the issue of rights and responsibilities is also one for government. The government has a right to expect compliance with those rules and regulations necessary for good order but it also has an onerous responsibility to ensure that the valid concerns of citizens are considered if not met and where social control is enforced for valid reasons rather than political dogma.

Perhaps there are two examples where this can be explored: Firstly, the planned introduction of identity cards. A quick look in almost everyone's wallet or purse will find an array of identity cards. The driving licence or the bank card are nothing more than identity cards that provide the holder to certain benefits. Of course we don't have to carry them but has anyone tried to get money out of a high street bank where they hold an account without a bankcard? Try leaving or, more importantly, entering the UK without a passport. These aren't simple pieces of identification; they are the tangible symbols of being on a number of databases. Only someone who has never worked legitimately, never travelled abroad or ever had need of medical services can survive without being included on computerized filing systems.

So why was the ID card scheme ultimately rejected (and rejected by a coalition Government who drew widespread public support from doing so)? Was it not because the infringement of rights became the battle cry rather than the responsibility of each of us to subject ourselves to a formal recording process. There was little dissent with the 2011 census because the need for this is well known and supported. What wasn't articulated to or accepted by the public with the ID card was the need for it.

In a society that, it is widely accepted, has become overburdened with rules and regulations the public are right to demand that only those things that are necessary for good order should be implemented. How many laws of the thousands created between 1997 and 2010 were really necessary or, if they were, was this necessity properly communicated to the public? Have we become a society strained by the responsibilities imposed by excessive regulation which, in turn, has caused a backlash focusing on rights?

The second area worthy of exploration touches on a sensitive area but one that politicians must be prepared to have an open and honest debate with the public. The UK has a long tradition of welcoming people to our shores. The rights of the visitor, be they casual holidaymakers, would be migrants or asylum seekers should be balanced by a responsibility to adhere to the social norms of the UK. We do not demand adherence, for example, to any religion but we do have the right to demand adherence to the laws of the country. The public does, rightly, question why someone who has come to this country is not required to leave if they break our laws. No one will suggest that low-level criminality should attract expulsion but someone who has been sentenced to a certain period of imprisonment should, unless there are compelling reasons why not, be deported at the end of their sentence.

There will be those who may find this suggestion at odds with their socialist principles, principles where the rights of the individual supported by human rights legislation have primacy over responsibilities to the state. However, there has to be a pragmatic approach to these delicate issues. The public demands, regardless of whether they have the right to demand, that government on their behalf or 'in their name' recognizes the incongruity of allowing the right to remain with the responsibility to deliver a safe society. If appeals are made on the grounds of 'right to family life' should this route be disbarred if there is any further serious criminality? These are the very real debates that must be undertaken and informed openly and transparently both within all parties and with the public at large.

It is widely accepted there is nothing wrong with imprisoning for a very long time the most dangerous of offenders. Indeed, the public expects that punishment is a part of any law and order regime just as much as rehabilitation. In a society that recognizes human frailties alongside out and out criminality we must continue to try and rehabilitate those who want to break out of the cycle of crime. Let's support those who want to break out of a cycle of drugs and crime by offering long term medical support. But when we reach the point where nothing is working or the offender rejects the opportunities we must be prepared to take tough decisions to protect society.

Therefore we have reached a point where debates over ideology have to take second place to the process of formulating policies that recognize the very real fears and concerns of the public. We might dream of a society where equality and fairness is the norm but we have to recognize that within the current financially focused system this might not be achievable. We might strive to eliminate poverty but we have to accept that there is always going to be a divide between rich and poor, between their different aspirations and between the strong willed and the feckless, and that these divides and the unfairness of a fully capitalist system will spawn envy and crime.

We might wish to further invest in a state education system that supports the achievers and develops to the best of their ability the less able, helping them to overcome the disadvantages of their background and family circumstances. We may wish to enhance the environment in which we live where those who take pride in their community and are prepared to work for it are rewarded.

We on the left need to recognize that to influence the future by forming a government the spin and rhetoric – the fine words – have to give way to pragmatic but achievable policies that can be put before the country. Where the links between the wider issues of society and crime, justice and law and order are put before the electorate and where they are encouraged to join the debate.

We must strive to redress the balance between the rights of the individual with their responsibilities towards their community – to acknowledge that rights fall out of responsibility and not the other way round.

We can't change the past – what's gone is gone – but we can influence the future and offer a future where individual rights are recognized in the context of each and every one of us to the state, society, our community and to each other.

Campaigning for Labour

Siôn Simon

Why Mayors Matter and Why Labour Should Support Them

Siôn stood down from Parliament last year in order to campaign for an elected Mayor of Birmingham. A former national newspaper columnist (most notably on the Daily Telegraph and the Spectator), he was Labour (and Unite) MP for Birmingham Erdington 2001-10, during which time he was first Further Education Minister then Minister for Creative Industries.

As well as demonstrating what central government can achieve towards Labour's objectives, the last government demonstrated its limits. If social democracy is to have a future it must be decentralised and pluralist, as concerned with social capital as with the resources of the state, and above all about mass mobilisation and mass innovation. This can't be delivered centrally. However, city leaders elected by the whole of their cities, with clear mandates for change, could and should achieve this mobilisation. President Bill Clinton said many times that "the era of big central government is over" and Labour should now be unambiguous about making the same point.

Labour is winning the big society debate by pointing out that the exit of the state doesn't necessarily mean that society will flourish. It's not about big government or big society. It's about what government and society can achieve together. While Labour is winning this debate, we still need to do much more to give life and definition to the kind of state that will be able to achieve most with society. As tribunes of civic pride and activism, mayors should be part of this answer. As such, due to the pride and activism that they tap into and direct, they should also feature in Labour thinking on identity.

Jon Cruddas is leading a debate on Labour and English identity. David Cameron is thrashing around in the debate on multiculturalism. The identity of cities is the missing link in both of these debates. Cities are where our different cultures come together. If Labour wants to avoid cultural, class and ethnic ghettos we need to articulate and actualise shared senses of being Brummie, Geordie or Scouse, etc, which transcend these groupings and bring our cities together. These shared city identities are bulwarks against extremism. It's true, as Cruddas argues, that if Labour can't capture a sense of Englishness then we vacate this territory to be defined by the right and the far right. But city identities are also important here because they are closer to the reality of how people perceive themselves and their lives.

These cities are wonderful, unique, living organisms. They have been harshly dealt with by a government that has no feeling or understanding for them. Perhaps the only thing this government has done for them is to provide the chance to fight back. That's what the opportunity to elect mayors amounts to. Labour should ensure that this chance is grasped. It is an opportunity not only to resist this vengeful and ideological government but to renew the partnerships that make up our cities. These are partnerships between those who came before us to create our cities, our children and grandchildren to whom we will bequeath our cities and ourselves. In this sense, mayors would be mere custodians of cities, creating the possibility that their cities may honour the memory of past generations and fulfil the obligations owed to future generations. For our cities to wither for want of such custodianship would be the cruellest betrayal.

There is plenty to resist in the Localism Bill. But we should welcome the provision for elected mayors in 11 English cities. It amounts to the logical progression of the devolution programme initiated by the last government. More mayors can address some of the cynicism that is felt about politics, achieve better policy and wrest some power downwards in what remains a heavily centralised state. And there is political advantage in more Labour mayors amplifying the voices against this destructive government.

Labour should be proud of our devolutionary actions – a Mayor for London and several smaller cities, assemblies for Northern Ireland and Wales and a Scottish Parliament. These were commonsense first steps in rebalancing the British state. We then took a wrong turn on the devolutionary road. Which is why mayoral city government has been much slower coming to the UK than almost everywhere else in the world. The referendum on a regional assembly for the north east confirmed that people rarely think of their region as a coherent civic unit in the way that they do their city.

The Tories were well set to take advantage of Labour's pulled punch, at a time when the appearance of dynamic modernity has been at a premium for them. But cowardice and incompetence led them incrementally to water down the Mayoral provisions of the Localism Bill – not the strongest prospectus to start with – almost beyond recognition. Good Mayors always accrete competences, though, and there remains just about enough in the Localism Bill for the version of mayoralty on offer to be a start that it certainly worth making.

Regionalism having foundered, devolution to our cities is the natural way forward in reconstructing our top-heavy state. Political institutions should reflect actual allegiances and identities, not artificial constructs. We spent years in government asking people to be grateful for the work of Regional

Development Agencies (RDAs) and the like. And some gratitude was merited. For most people, though, unelected, regional bodies are inherently an abstraction from who they are, while being Brummie, Geordie or Scouse is anything but. When, however, was the last time the people of these cities really came together to address the issues that matter to them?

This isn't what they are doing when their city council leaders are elected in secret by a handful of councillors from their party group. Nor is it what they are doing when most of them do not even know the name of either the leader or the chief executive pulling their strings. Cities will only recapture command of their destinies when we collectively decide who leads us and on the basis of what manifesto. City-wide dialogue and choice makes mayoral systems more vibrant and democratic than the status quo, which too often amounts to self-selecting elites talking to themselves to justify their failings.

In his 2011 Lunar Society lecture, Andrew Adonis asked the great and good of Birmingham to reflect upon what their city has become. The Lib Dem deputy leader of the council did all he could to stop the speech from even being made. If those presently responsible for running our cities can be dragged away from their cocooned other-worlds, they might be made to see sharply divergent economic performance. While Brighton and Milton Keynes both grew their private sector job bases by 25 percent between 1998 and 2008, some cities slipped backwards: Stoke (-16 percent), Blackburn (-12 percent), Blackpool (-6 percent).[6] The UK's economic imbalances are correlated with one of the most centralised political systems in the democratic world. To what extent this extends to causation is debatable. But those who advocate localism – a decentralisation of political power – as being good for the economy concede at least some causation. And we all claim to be localists now.

But there is genuine and sham localism. Labour should campaign for the former and expose the latter. This requires that

Labour hold localism proposals to the real localism standards proposed by IPPR – that localism be effective and efficient; properly funded; at the heart of a drive for social justice; accompanied by a step-change in the transparency and accountability of local decision-making; and framed within a constitutional settlement between central and local government.[7] These standards matter because you can't be serious about having a strategy for growth unless you are serious about having a strategy for rebalancing the economy and you can't be serious about rebalancing the economy unless you are serious about rebalancing political power.

Real localists are aghast not only that the Regional Growth Fund is one quarter the size of the 2009/10 budget for the (now abolished) RDAs but at the extent of central control over the much more substantial mainstream budgets. Regional development funds account for less than one percent of total government spending in the regions.[8] Mainstream budgets, such as transport, skills and housing, are much larger. The transparency and accountability of mayors creates a legitimate basis for the principles of real localism to be increasingly applied to these budgets.

Where our last period in opposition saw the sprouting of the loony left in local government; now local government should see the emergence of the next generation of Labour leaders. Lambeth, which then gave us Red Ted Knight, now pioneers the ground-breaking co-operative council model. Liverpool was then troubled by Militant yet could soon have a dynamic, intelligent voice in national policy debates in the form of a Labour mayor. That Andrew Adonis, as Transport Secretary, reports struggling to understand the views of great regional cities, while the Mayor of London relentlessly bent his ear, is indicative of how mute our regional cities have been.[9]

Name recognition of mayors in the north eastern cities which have them is 73 per cent. The average for council leaders in leader/cabinet areas is 25 per cent, much less in larger cities. Name recognition and visibility creates the basis for increased public accountability and cycles of engagement. Of course, this alone will not redeem politics, but it will help. Politics is meant to be about people coming together to address shared concerns. Too often, though, people have no idea which branch of government is responsible for the issues important to them. This isn't their fault, obviously. It is politics that is wrong, not people.

Democracy only works when there is an identifiable someone to hold to account, and a direct means of doing so. For much more of our politics mayors can be that person, particularly if a dose of real localism were to be applied to more mainstream budgets. Now, the person really in charge is someone hundreds of miles away in Whitehall, who has never been elected by anyone and never even been questioned by the Public Accounts Committee, never mind on a doorstep.

That most of the public policy that applies to most of the country is devised and implemented centrally can mean that localities experience policy that doesn't have sufficient regard for their particular needs and capabilities and so goes against the grain of the best public policy. Mayors would give cities a mandate for policy to be more rooted in the people and places that make up these cities. This combined with the increased accountability of mayors will make for better public policy.

The best policy in one city may look quite different from that in another city. Labour's federalists need to win out against its centralisers for the virtues of this plurality to be fully appreciated by the party. G.D.H. Cole said: "There have always been two fundamental cleavages in socialist thought – the cleavage between revolutionaries and reformists, and the cleavage between centralisers and federalists".[10] The reformists won the first battle. The second battle continues. It's important to Labour's revival that the federalists win. Labour mayors have a big part to play.

Joseph Russo

Co-ops and New Labour

Joseph is vice chair of Dumfriesshire Clydesdale & Tweeddale CLP and a long time Credit Union & Co-operative activist. He is also a Co-operative Party Organiser and writes in a personal capacity.

Since its beginnings New Labour always struggled with notions of common ownership. By the time Tony Blair pushed through changes to Clause IV, common ownership had, despite the best efforts of the Webbs, become synonymous with public ownership where the state owned key industries and provided public services directly through monolithic bureaucracies.

Tony Blair was right to sense that a modern political party, one which hoped to have the broad appeal necessary to propel it into government, could not be weighed down by an ideological heritage which the fall of the Berlin Wall seemed to indicate had failed. Indeed the fall of communism famously heralded the 'end of history' according to political scientist Francis Fukuyama and therefore necessitated a paradigm shift for Labour, started under Kinnock and completed under Blair.

The mistake of New Labour however, was to view all that went before as an irrelevance. Labour, widely viewed as being founded solely by the trade unions was at the time of its foundation deeply entrenched in a much wider realm of civic society. A civic society determined to better themselves and society at large.

One aspect of this wider civic society was the Co-operative Society. At one time every town and village had its own Co-operative Society providing affordable, untainted food and often communities would also start friendly societies to provide for their welfare in times of need too. Both of these community mutuals were built on a noble working class tradition of collective self help.

At the time of the Rochdale Pioneers (1844) the co-operative principles of self-help, self-responsibility, democracy, equality, equity and solidarity were utterly revolutionary, they still are today, which is why the Co-operative Group is running an advertising campaign called 'Join the Revolution'. They are still revolutionary because they demand the injection of democracy into the world of business and public policy where so often we are led to believe they don't belong.

Whether it's a retail co-operative owned by its members or a paper mill owned by its workers, democracy and the empowerment of communities is at the heart of the co-op movement. Co-operators believe that any group of people with a dash of diversity can and will come to correct and logical decisions even without expert knowledge. A firm belief that the man in Whitehall does not always know best and that local communities are best placed to take the decisions that directly affect them and their welfare.

In 1917 Co-operative Congress agreed that the co-operative movement needed political representation and established what shortly thereafter became the Co-operative Party. The party contested elections alone until the 1928 Cheltenham agreement when it was decided that the Co-operative Party and Labour

Party, both being parties of the working class should work together. From this point on the Co-operative Party has been the sister party of Labour fighting for social justice and arguing the case for mutualism.

It can hardly be surprising that the two parties came to work together; both were largely working class and socialist and though there were always differences it made little sense to have two largely similar parties chasing the same vote.

By the time that the Attlee government was swept to power in a wave of post-war euphoria the Co-op retail societies were, though individually often quite small (with exceptions including Royal Arsenal Co-op in London which along with a few others affiliated to the Labour Party directly & not the Co-op Party), collectively formed the biggest retail group in Britain with market share that peaked at over 30% in the 1950s. The same market share as Tesco today.

This perceived power, combined with a view that the movement was somehow to the right of the unions made them and the Labour Party nervous, leading to a re-negotiation of the two parties' pact. This distracted the party at a time of great opportunity when it could have been arguing more vigorously for co-operative and mutual solutions to the issues of the day. The National Insurance Act 1911, the foundation stone of the welfare state, was essentially the Liberal Party copying with some differences the insurance-based welfare system used in Germany. It mandated the payment of insurance contributions into mutual Friendly Societies. Whilst the Germans have gone on to build upon a similar system to create universality of service, the National Health Service Act did away with all that bringing the entire system in house and under the direction of the Secretary of State.

The result today is an admirable system built on sound moral principles but it is also a system liable to become a political football, a system with almost no democratic controls and one with poorer outcomes by international measures than the German system. The NHS is the easiest example to single out but there are many more. And while social democratic parties used co-operative models to great effect on the continent we in the UK stuck to command and control models which centralised rather than democratised.

Unfortunately for the Co-operative Party and the wider movement, the great moderniser Tony Blair, recognised that the command and control model was, in a post-perestroika era, not one with any further mileage. Equally though, in 1997 the UK co-operative sector was not in good health.

Once the dominant force on the high street the movement had failed to modernise and keep up with consumer tastes, and had fallen behind privately held competitors. In some cases too, its belated desire to improve efficiency had been at the cost of its democratic roots. In London the situation was particularly bad; important for informing the political classes. And with wave after wave of societies failing and merging together the sector was left looking anaemic and was struggling with its own internal problems.

Throughout the 80s and into the 90s, carpet baggers had forced demutualisation of several big name building societies, persuading members that cash in the pocket was more desirable than social solidarity and the public good. Abbey National was the first to demutualise, Halifax the largest and Northern Rock the last big society and most ill-fated.

Hardly surprising then, that Tony Blair, desperate to find a message to resonate with 'Middle England', was hardly enthusiastic about a model of governance which looked like a cloth capped, working class failure. Tony, who recognised that there had been a paradigm shift in public perceptions of the state, was grasping for the alternative but did not embrace co-operatives as a solution.

In some ways the creation of social enterprise and its various corporate structures was a massive reinvention of the co-operative wheel. Social enterprise was a method of non-political social action, an anodyne attempt to strip the politics from the inherently political. But at the same time it did lead to the creation of many grass roots co-operatives: A real increase in the size and scope of community credit unions, an attempt to re-inject some democracy into the NHS using Foundation Trusts and many other examples which have served as a springboard for a co-operative renaissance.

Sadly, the full fruits of this renaissance have ripened slightly too late for Labour to have grasped wholeheartedly in government. And, though the 2010 Labour manifesto was full of Co-operative Party policies, it was unable to convince the electorate that it ought to be returned for a fourth term.

The Co-operative Group and its retail empire, the most visible part of the movement to the casual observer, has been transformed since 1997. The Co-operative Bank has become a market leader in ethical finance and has stood unscathed by the world financial crisis. The Group has not only consolidated and rebranded but also expanded merging in Britannia Building Society with the bank and buying up Somerfield, moving the Co-operative towards a double digit market share for the first time in decades. Meanwhile John Lewis, essentially an employee owned Co-operative, has expanded and become the favourite department store of the upwardly aspirational middle classes.

With such a spectacular turnaround in business fortunes, coinciding with the return of the retail dividend and re-invigorated democratic structures it's little wonder that the movement has also attracted attention from those not traditionally supportive of the co-operative ethos.

Having shed its working class down-at-heel image the business model has attracted new fans in a Conservative Party desperate to reform its image. David Cameron's 'Big Society' clearly acknowledges the worth of co-operative enterprises in communities and sees the clear scope for public service delivery along co-operative lines.

The Conservatives have already outlined plans to hive off government functions to worker co-operatives which sounds like a great idea in some respects but as with the whole 'Big Society' agenda it is a proposal predicated upon the need to cut government expenditure, lacking in clear safeguards for these new co-operative enterprises against de-mutualisation, redundancies and prejudicial procurement practices' all indicating a lack of understanding of the model they feign enthusiasm for and belies their alternative motives.

The Conservatives agenda is to shrink the size and cost of the State by usurping the co-operative business model. They mistakenly believe that a co-operative is a cut price option rather than a co-operative being an added value option. Added value through the application of co-operative values and principles which include the redistribution of profits and a concern for the community and such un-conservative notions as solidarity.

Labour must grasp this added value principle. Co-operatives put people at the heart of their business. Co-operatives are not necessarily the cheapest option for public service delivery but when done correctly they are a quality option adding democracy, accountability and a degree of autonomy.

To move towards regaining the trust of the British people, and ultimately power, we as a Labour movement need to re-interpret our old dogmas embracing our communitarian and pre-Marxist roots. Labour must construct a new narrative which both empowers the working classes and reassures the middle classes.

There needs to be recognition that the collective welfare of the people ought to be above party politics and as a social good in and of itself be protected from electoral whim. Our social democratic sister parties in mainland Europe have long recognised this. For them, co-operative structures as the means of service delivery are commonplace because they recognise that they will not always be in power. As a consequence vital services and social programmes need to be kept at arms length from the state. They insulate key services from party political whim using networks of independent mutuals providing healthcare, social housing, welfare *and* user accountability.

We need to be looking at the thoughts of Robert Owen, Pierre-Joseph Proudhon and José Maria Arizmendiarrieta (founder of Mondragon) both to inform a new mutualist narrative for Labour which will provide employment and regenerate communities whilst exposing the big society as a ghoulish and misanthropic fig leaf which uses the language of the left to justify the cuts of the right.

Indeed in a mutual future the state would still have a crucial role to play in the provision of finance and as a guarantor of rights and services. Even today the state provides many local mutual start-ups with soon-to-be-cut finance. Mutualism offers a much needed new narrative for Labour. It engages the grassroots and recognises the electorate's suspicion of the state without embracing neo-liberal economics. Mutualism encourages self help without abolishing state help. Co-operatives empower communities, can improve services and allow for local solutions to local problems. Mutualism is the future of socialism and a new, real alternative for the Labour Party to embrace and to lead it back to power.

Bill Esterson MP

A Campaigning Party

Bill is the MP for Sefton Central, who was first elected to Parliament in 2010. He is a member of the Education Select Committee and is on the National Policy Forum. He served for 15 years as a Councillor in Medway, and was up until May 2010, the opposition spokesman for children's services. Previously he was Director of Leaps and Bounds Training which specialises in the design of management and communications skills.

The Labour Party was founded as a campaigning party to address issues in the workplace and in the community. In the workplace those issues covered pay, conditions, health and safety. In the community the issues covered public health and housing. The appeal of the party and of the Labour movement was based on fighting for the people who needed help, the many not the few. It was also based on gaining the support of people in the workplace and in the community by talking to those people, by listening to the issues of concern to them and by showing people that Labour and trade union representatives could be trusted and were on the side of the people. We were very much the people's party as well as the workers' party. There are still far too many cases of poor public health and substandard housing, not to mention poor safety and conditions in the workplace.

Although conditions are far removed from those of the late 19th century and quality of life and life expectancy is far better today.

The Labour movement was largely responsible for the transformation which led from the nasty, brutish and often short, Hobbesian lives lived by many in the Victorian era to the relative comfort and health of the early 21st century. Improvements happened for the many under the recent Labour government which lasted for far longer than any of its predecessors, whether those improvements were in decent homes standards, child tax credits, a minimum wage, Sure Start or dramatically shorter NHS waiting lists. And the very fact that we have had an NHS for over 60 years is testament to the values and ideals of the founding members of our movement.

The last Labour government had many fine achievements but for many those achievements were undermined by activities which were not consistent with what happened when Labour was founded. Iraq, ID cards, the dependence on expensive sources of finance for new hospitals and schools. All have their critics and are areas that are worthy of re-evaluation. To that list we should add our all too cosy relationship with media tycoons.

In my constituency of Sefton Central, it is clear that many people have done very well in recent years. People have prosperity and well-being which would have been unimaginable 120 years ago. And yet, a few miles down the road in Bootle, life expectancy is a staggering 10 years lower than in the relatively prosperous towns of Crosby, Formby and Maghull.

When I knock on doors in Central Sefton, people ask me for help with housing, with environmental issues (not a million miles from the public health matters of long ago) and are worried about job security, pay and conditions at work. It seems to me that the issues of concern today are often the not so distant relations of either the workplace or the community issues of the 1890s. In fact given the deregulation and the race to the bottom which Tory policy is heading towards. Safety at work is likely to re-establish itself alongside pay and conditions as a key issue if that has not already happened. The threat to pensions and to living standards is also a threat to public health and housing as people will not be able to afford their current standard of living and the shortage of housing will make life very hard for many more people. Witness the evidence that up to 40,000 families will be made homeless by changes to benefits rules.

Our challenge then is to recognise that we had good reasons for championing the issues which were prominent in the 1890s. We were an effective campaigning organisation at that time albeit in a different society to that of 2011.

In our history, we have been at our best when we have campaigned. Whether for pay and conditions, better housing, free education (as opposed to so-called Free Schools) and the NHS. And whether it has been Labour candidates seeking election or re-election or support for policies in power or on the road to power, the process has always succeeded because the public has supported our programme. That has only ever come through taking our case to the people. Trade union members face a fight for their livelihoods against the cuts and against a Tory government hell bent on cutting too fast and too far for the good of the people of this country in the short term and in the interests only of their friends who wait to make money out of the crisis. The Tory former Home Secretary, David Davies, describes the capitalist system as one of wealth extraction and he is right in his analysis. The Tory party operates in a way which maximises that wealth extraction. The banking system, private health companies and outsourcers who run services for councils, all of these are geared to making profits which go to a few shareholders or senior managers at the expense of the many in their organisations and beyond. Wealth extraction for the few, not the many, is light years from the wealth creation which the One Nation Tories of the past espoused.

Well organised trade unionists have taken their campaigns outside the workplace and into the communities to win the support of the public. Campaigns have been to highlight the effects of wealth extraction on living standards of both the staff who face cuts in pay and conditions and on the public who face a drop in the quality of services. When trades union members have had the support of the public they have been successful. Bus drivers in London leafleted extensively and won the support of their passengers by talking to them. As a result, when UNITE organised strike action, the drivers had overwhelming public support. In my constituency, in Formby the teachers have gone door to door and leafleted residents about the plans of the two High Schools to convert to academies. That means awareness about the issue, about the downside to leaving local authority control and about the long term impact on children and on the wider community. If teachers then feel the need to take action they will have support from the wider public.

Campaigning is effective when it leads to the public being persuaded. The Tories can and do back down in the face of public opinion. Take circus animals or forests or NHS reform. All subject to humiliating U-turns by Cameron and co. All on the back of massive public campaigns where public opinion was firmly against the government. It can be done by workers under threat of losing pensions rights. It can be done by teachers who are undermined by the Secretary of State who thinks teacher training is unnecessary and it can be done by council staff who know that the most vulnerable will suffer if the cuts are pushed through in social care. Cameron will provoke people into strikes if he thinks the rest of the public do not understand the issues. He wants union members to strike because he thinks he will win the public relations battle. Cameron and Osborne see strikes as a trap for working people which will undermine public support. This is not necessarily the case. If union members win the hearts and minds and the Tories don't back down, in the face of public opinion, then industrial action can be effective. If workers strike without public support, however, the danger is that a dispute becomes a battle where the public tend to believe the media and the record of the media is not one which favours our side of the argument.

The Labour Party only became an effective political force when working people started to campaign for it in their communities. This is an important lesson for today. For the unions to win on behalf of their members, campaigning is crucial, in the workplace, on the doorstep and in the media. So too for Labour candidates. When both parts of the Labour movement work together, we are far more powerful. There are 3 million levy payers who are union members. Yet most are not engaged with the political section of the movement, the Labour Party. Many don't vote Labour or at least didn't last year. Drawing on the potential of the support in the unions and the potential for activity in our communities of involving some of the levy payers is a natural and important opportunity for the party and for the unions. United we are strong. Divided (by the Tories and their friends in the media) we are weak.

Winning hearts and minds applies to people with workplace disputes. It also applies to those of us who are elected. The reality is that winning hearts and minds is a very time consuming and long term process. Last year in the general election, Labour performed best where it did most knocking on doors, made the most phone calls and delivered the most leaflets. Both in the years before the election and in the short campaign just before election day. This is because of human nature. People respond to messages which are repeated again and again and again. It's why companies advertise the same messages again and again and again. Most people don't go out looking for marketing messages and don't take much notice of them when they hear them. We are delivering a marketing message whether it's a group of workers trying to improve their pay and conditions or Labour candidates seeking election. We are competing with the soap manufacturers and car dealerships for attention. So we have to repeat our messages over and over again to get through, influence and convince. I said we always campaigned. We did. We were effective in the 1890s because there was not so much other marketing around. The lesson is that we have to campaign hard to win in the workplace or on the doorstep.

The amount of work involved in successful campaigning is not to be underestimated. We have few active campaigners. In the places where we lost our MPs last year or in 2005 there is often very little in the way of activity because there are so few people to do the work. The party must address this issue if it is to stand any chance of winning in 2015. The Tories appointed local organisers in their key seats in 2005. This approach paid off for them in 2010. We must do the same in 2011 to win in 2015.

. In the run up to the 1997 election, we became an effective campaigning organisation. We won seats in places where Labour had never won largely because of a huge amount of work and organisation by an army of volunteers, with support from trade union branches. The party was quite cautious in its plans pre-1997. It targeted a relatively limited number of seats to ensure victory and a working majority. Labour won every one of its target seats through excellent local and national organisation. Our media operation was outstanding and the regional staff performed superbly. The level of activity inspired volunteers on the ground and that included in non-target seats. I campaigned in Medway where I lived. Medway was not a target seat. Neither were Chatham and Aylesford or Gillingham. Yet we won all three of the seats which cover the Medway Towns. This was due to the efforts of the volunteers in those seats, the candidates and their teams. Regional office was able to provide limited support but most of the work came from the individual campaigns themselves. In 1997 we were able to organise at a local level. We had the people with the skills and the resources to win.

So can we repeat our success in 1997? I believe we can. We need the right vision and the right policies. But if we have the right organisation, we can achieve a huge amount as we proved in 1997 and in 2010. There are a number of steps which we must take now. We have to revitalise the activity at a local level. A key ingredient is having full time organisers in key seats. The party must raise funds specifically to pay for good quality organisers. Those organisers need to build up the activity in key seats. It is clear to me that this is not going to happen overnight and that is a reason for starting straight away. The evidence from 1997 and 2010 is the same. Where we knocked on the most doors, phoned the most people, delivered the most leaflets and had the best local media coverage, we had the best results. This sounds obvious because it is obvious but it takes a huge amount of work and that work can only be done by a very large number of people.

So how do we go from the current absence of volunteers to a situation like the one we had in 1997? The local organisers will need to recruit many volunteers. Some will be party members, but not all. In fact, many people who deliver leaflets for us don't want to join the party but they are happy doing what they see as their bit. Gisela Stuart tells me that in Edgbaston she had about 100 volunteers, many of whom were not party members. She has found over the years that by helping community groups and individuals over and over again, those same people are delighted to help with leafleting and sometimes with other activities like knocking on doors. I have found that when I find enthusiastic Labour supporters on the doorstep or on the phone, it is worth asking if they want to get involved.

Recruiting volunteers is a big part of our organisational effort. We also need to keep hold of our volunteers and members once they become involved. That means saying thank you and including them in social events as well as campaign events.

Some people reading my comments might think I believe the Labour Party is just about winning elections. I happen to think the party is about a lot more than winning elections. However, political parties exist to win and exercise power. That is why a Labour Party was created in the first place, although campaigning and raising issues was a key part of why the party was set up, ultimately it was created so that representatives could be elected to push the policies needed by working people.

The Labour Party is an organisation of 200,000 members. The party is its members and those members decide how it operates and what its policies are. That's the theory anyway. The practice is in reality a compromise. We elect a leader and officers at all levels of the party to carry out the duties of the party. When the Labour Party was set up it was based on a set of values. The values of the Labour Party today have evolved from those of the 1890s but the party should still use its founding principles as the basis for how it operates. More recently we can learn from our time in government. We can celebrate successes such as a minimum wage and Sure Start and, for many, the creation of the NHS remains our finest achievement. However, we can also learn from decisions taken in government which might have been different, such as on foreign policy or on the private finance initiative.

We succeeded in the run up to the 1997 election for a number of reasons, our organisation, our leadership, the state of the Tories after 18 years all had their part to play. When it came to policy we had 5 simple pledges. They were easy to implement so we could not be accused of promising and then not delivering on those promises. This approach has the advantage that it cannot be used against us by our opponents as an example of reckless spending. Learning from the approach (if not necessarily from the policies) some simple pledges can be devised to reconnect with the public on policies which are of greatest concern to them. On crime, on jobs, on housing, on schools and on health, policies would give us a way of capturing the mood of the public just as we did in 1997. It is also important to start to create an early narrative that assures people that we are on their side now.

For people to have confidence that they can elect a Labour government in 2015 they need to see evidence that we are in step with them from now onwards and that we have moved on from the areas where we were out of step and did not appear to understand what was important to the voters in the years before the 2010 election. Immigration is an example of how we failed to respond to the public mood and where we need a coherent narrative. One idea would be the use of minimum wage legislation to make sure that employers cannot bring in foreign workers to undercut local people in the jobs market. Enforcement also means resources for agencies like HMRC. The cuts by the Tories to HMRC are just one of many examples where the consequences have far reaching, damaging effects for people on low and middle incomes which go beyond the immediate effect on the families of those losing their jobs in the public sector. Enforcement of minimum wage legislation is one example that addresses concerns on immigration. It appeals to the sense of fairness which most people feel is missing in many areas.

A combination of organisation and simple policy ideas is an approach for our party which can draw on our values and it is an approach which will appeal to the hard working people on low and middle incomes of this country. We can appeal to the sense of fairness of the British people through the narrative we create now. They will respond to the Labour Party if we show that we are on their side. In order to show that we understand, we will need to be active in our communities and show that we support people in their everyday struggles. We need to give people a reason to vote for us in 2015. People will vote for us if we prove by our actions as well as our words that we are on their side. That means being an active, community based, campaigning organisation, which responds to the issues which people care about. It also means having the simple policies which show we are in touch.

Those policies will be about the issues which matter most to those who face tough times from having their living standards squeezed.

The Rt Hon David Hanson MP
What Awaits Labour in 2015?

David was elected to represent Delyn, Wales in the 1992 election; he has served in government under both Blair and Brown and has held several government positions including as PPS to Tony Blair, Parliamentary Under Sec for Wales, and as a Minister at the Ministry of Justice, The Northern Ireland Office and at The Home Office. David is currently a Shadow Treasury Minister.

The values of the Welsh Labour party have had a major influence on UK Labour policy over the last 100 years and I believe they will continue to do so. However, with a changing electorate, less wedded to traditional party loyalties, Welsh Labour, as with UK Labour will need, once more, to make those values relevant to the next generation. In Wales, with Labour in opposition in Westminster and in government in Wales, we now have a historic opportunity to work together for victory at the next election.

For over a hundred years the voice of Labour and the voice of Wales have spoken as one. From our party's founders with Keir Hardie's election as MP for Merthyr Tydffil in 1906 to Ramsay MacDonald, later to be Labour's first Prime Minister as MP for

Aberavon, Labour has been the champion of Wales and the aspiration of the Welsh people.

Long before David Cameron's big society was even thought of, communities across Wales have for decades practised a socialism that pre-dated that concept with book clubs, music, education and a community of spirit and action.

The trade union movement rooted in heavy industry like coal, steel and in public services was as strong in Wales as in any part of the United Kingdom. Labour's role, in representing working people, arguing for change and moving social progress forward was key in the social changes of the 20th century. Whilst having a unique identity, the Welsh Labour movement has always been internationalist and outward looking, opposing fascism and building strong international links.

The foundation of the National Health Service, one of Labour's greatest achievements, grew as a response to the kind of social problems that were rife in Nye Bevan's Ebbwr Vale. And with our leaders Jim Callaghan, Michael Foot, and Neil Kinnock representing Welsh seats in Parliament – Labour was in tune with the aspirations of Wales for most of the 20th century and took the values of our movement in Wales to the heart of our party and government.

I am proud to have, at home, the first election address that Ramsay MacDonald stood on. Although he later left Labour, and Wales, it is worth noting the programme we fought on in those early days. Central to it was devolution for Wales, a minimum wage and reform of the Lords. Pledges eventually carried through by the 1997 Labour Government, based on values that are universal and relevant today.

It was Labour who founded the Welsh Assembly and in the recent referendum who led the vote for a resounding 'yes' to strengthened powers. Time after time it has been Welsh Labour that has led the way in Wales articulating and delivering for its people. The values of social justice, respect and equality of opportunity were and are in the blood of the Welsh Labour movement.

Yet that history is just that – history. Wales does not owe Labour a vote in perpetuity, nothing is set in stone and we certainly do not have a right to rule. That changing face of Wales has given momentum to the changing face of political life.

As recently as the early 1990s, my constituency employed 2,000 miners – not any more. The 20,000 steel workers employed in North East Wales in 1980, now much reduced, still producing high quality goods but not on the industrial scale of the past. Across Wales the old industrial base has changed and with it the guaranteed loyalty of thousands of individual voters. We need to work harder for our votes. We, in North Wales, as in much of the rest of Wales, now have our employment base from hi-tech skills, green jobs, retail and tourism, as much as from the manufacturing industry and the public sector – and that change is one which Labour has to keep pace with.

Labour in local government, had its worst result in Wales in 2008 for a generation – two councils out of 22 remain under Labour control. Whilst still dominant, the lowest number of councillors in living memory. There are now more independent councillors in Wales than there are Labour councillors. Next year in the local elections we have an opportunity to take back some key councils, but this won't be easy.

At the last Westminster election in 2010 Labour's share of the vote was at 36 percent, the lowest in any election since 1918. Worse even than the very difficult election of 1983, when perhaps Labour was saved in Wales by having a Labour MP, Michael Foot MP as its leader, and by the traditional loyalties to our party.

After 13 years of Government, that election was always going to be a challenge, but coupled with the decline of the trade union base, the growing aspiration of the middle class in Wales and a resurgent Conservative party, that challenge was made all the more difficult.

Since 2010 the Assembly election has seen the recapturing of some of that ground by Labour, who are now solely in government with 30 seats. The fact that Wales has the only Labour administration in the UK is not only a real challenge, but a real opportunity as I will explore later on.

With the election of a Conservative Government, supported by the Liberal Democrats in Westminster, new challenges are now emerging. Already with the boundary review the number of Parliamentary seats in Wales is set to be reduced from 40 to 30 – with a possible knock on effect to the Assembly boundaries in the future. Fewer Welsh MPs at Westminster makes the need for Labour to speak with one clear and effective voice even more important. That knock-on effect to the Assembly boundaries raises the challenge for Labour, which has already been discussed by the Shadow Secretary of State, Peter Hain, who has sought a revised Assembly of 30 two member seats elected by first past the post for the next Assembly election if 2016.

The Tory approach to the role of Welsh MPs seems to be one of marginalisation. It's clear to me that the real Tory wish is to reduce the role of Welsh MPs in a UK Government so as to deny us a vote on areas that are important to Wales. This is problematic when you consider that the Welsh budgets are still controlled by Westminster and that, in a constituency like mine, thousands of constituents work and use public services over in England. Such a move from this government would, by stealth, make Wales ever more distant from the heart of UK Government where we still need to be heard.

By coincidence, this chimes nicely with the nationalist agenda of a separate Wales where the so-called benign influence of the United Kingdom will be removed to allow Wales to determine its own destiny. Of course this neatly forgets the economic and social imperative of maintaining a strong union, which Labour should take every opportunity to champion.

As for the Liberal Democrats, their actions in propping up this

Tory Government means they have forfeited the right to represent progressive politics in Wales. So in the run up to the next general election, Labour will face the twin track of defending Wales against the Tory-Lib Dem Government and painting a clear alternative on devolved issues, whilst at the same time making a case for a strong union and an active representation in Westminster.

In achieving this I see a number of key challenges that need to be tackled. Firstly there needs to be a value led approach and a clear, strong Labour message in the Assembly; echoing values of social justice, equality of opportunity and strong and active communities.

Labour leader Carwyn Jones and his team have made a good start. In winning back control of the Welsh Assembly they are focusing on Labour's historic tasks of ensuring opportunity, access to services and safer communities.

In its manifesto earlier this year, candidates for the Welsh Assembly stood for more apprenticeships and training opportunities for our young people; better access to GP surgeries; more funding for our schools; more police community support officers for safer communities; and a commitment to double the number of children benefiting from free childcare and health visiting. All are forward looking and draw inspiration from the Labour movement.

Whilst committing to more investments Labour in Wales recognised that in these straightened times they would have to do more to protect policies and initiatives which came forward over the last 13 years. These included free prescriptions, free bus travel for pensioners and disabled people and their carers; free school breakfasts and school milk for the under 7s and support for Welsh students so they will not have to pay higher tuition fees. Finally, and in recognition of the employment challenges in Wales, a commitment to build on the successful ReAct programme.

In these financially more difficult times we need to do this in an ever more efficient manner, looking for cost savings, protecting the frontline and showing the Conservative Government in Westminster that efficient public services can be undertaken, without the short sighted, too-far too-fast, approach of the UK Tories. All of these commitments show the difference a Labour Government can make in the Assembly.

Increasingly as the Tory-led Government develop their free market approach to health and education in particular, the alternative of the Welsh Assembly will both be tested under Conservative attacks and become more relevant to the needs of people in Wales. The Conservative attack on public spending disproportionately hits Wales where we are more reliant on the public sector and where the painful transition will be felt that much harder. The decision to cut too far and too fast is a politically motivated one, the economic consequences of which remain to be seen.

Already we have seen the Tories attack the approach of the Welsh Assembly. As we get closer to the General Election, the focus is now on Labour in Wales, as the only remaining national Labour Government in the United Kingdom. How it performs, will impact not only those of us that live in Wales, but on the perception of a competent potential government in the United Kingdom.

Central to getting our message across will mean co-operation between the Labour led assembly and the Labour party across the UK and in Westminster. There are clear tasks for us in articulating that future.

Firstly, whilst we should be proud of our record on devolution and proud of what Labour's agenda is achieving in Wales in the face of Conservative attacks on that record and nationalist attacks on the limitations of the Assembly. Our task is to prove that the current devolution settlement works and that further changes to it, either from the Tory right or the nationalist wing will do damage to the people of Wales.

Secondly, we need to articulate the benefits of being part of the United Kingdom, and recognise the contribution that being part of that United Kingdom brings to Wales.

The interdependence of the UK and Wales is self-evident. Some of the biggest industries in Wales, such as Airbus, close to my constituency, are multi-national, thriving entities that need support from the Assembly but also need the weight of the UK Government to help them compete on a global level. Our economy, our taxation and our criminal justice system, defence, social security and much of our transport system remains the responsibility of the UK Government and we need to be at the centre of that decision making process. The challenges of tackling long-term unemployment and regeneration, have to be done in partnership between the Assembly and Westminster. The Labour agenda in Wales should reflect the need for this strong partnership, based on our common values between the Wales and the UK Labour party.

Thirdly, through a close working relationship with our external partners, we can invest in and develop energy alternatives, attract new industry to Wales and re-skill our young people. Only through that partnership can Wales prosper. We need to compete with the world – a world that quite frankly we remain on the edge of. That means a revolution in our approach to new technology, skill development and the innovation that led to Wales growing the industrial revolution in the first place.

As history has shown, Wales has always done things in its own way but has looked outwards beyond its borders– an internationalist agenda. To do this successfully, it must work with the Labour party in the UK and in Westminster.

In order to deliver all of this, we need to be in tune with the aspiration of the people of Wales. Like the Labour Party across the whole of the United Kingdom that means we need an active community based Labour membership where we attract the people. These people display our values in their communities on a day to day basis, and should join our party and reflect those values and aspirations at a town, county, region, Welsh or UK level.

So the future challenge for Labour in Wales, first and foremost, is to remember the values that have driven it to its successes in the 20th Century, grounded in those of Keir Hardie back in 1906; opportunity for all, social justice, community. We will grow and win the next election in Wales and elsewhere by being clear on this future challenge. In Wales that means a strong Labour message in the Assembly, but one that links with the UK Government and builds on that strength. Wales must continue to look outward – strong on its responsibilities, but confident in its role in the UK and wider world.

Eric Joyce MP

It's a SIN

Eric Joyce is a former soldier, and was elected to Parliament as MP for Falkirk West in 2000 and is now MP for Falkirk. He is Chair (Digital) of PICTFOR and The African Great Lakes Group and is a former Chair of The Fabian Society for whom he edited; "Now's The Hour – New Thinking for Holyrood".

Imagine a 'Scottish Independent Nation' which raises and spends most of its own public cash and, with important caveats, opts in to major UK institutions where the Scottish public feels it's in our interests. The Bank of England sets common interest rates for Scotland until, perhaps, we all enter the Euro on some distant horizon. The HMRC collects taxes. Primary financial regulation extends from London's powerful place in the world financial system. A common armed services reflects common strategic and practical imperatives. A federated British Broadcasting Corporation sees a Scottish Broadcasting Commission ensure more programmes are produced in Scotland but also remain part of one of the largest and most potent media brands in the world. Less well known but nevertheless key institutions such as communications regulator OFCOM, the

DVLA and Ordnance Survey continue to serve Scotland, England, Wales and Northern Ireland but on an opt-in basis and with renewed governance structures. Scottish MPs still serve Scotland's interests at Westminster. The Queen remains head of state. The language of autonomy and independence of spirit dominates but the union remains strong, if different.

This 'devolution max', or 'independence-lite' if you will, not outright independence, will be the essence of the main pitch made by the Scottish National Party during the 3 or so years before the 'independence' referendum. It's also what Scotland will choose; the question put in the referendum will be designed to facilitate that outcome.

Right now, less than 30% of people living in Scotland favour outright independence; around the same figure favour the status quo. That means an overwhelming majority want greater devolution, either as a first choice or, in the case of the pro-independence folk, a gradational second choice. But for now, Labour's official position on devolution is to defend the status quo; to present the dangers of 'independence' ad nauseam. Few find that position authentic. With the SNP off to a fast start, we're still on the starting blocks.

Academics and lawyers are already arguing that the SNP needs to come off the fence; that 'devolution max' or 'independence lite' is neither fish nor foul. I think the opposite is true. SNP orthodoxy is now to argue theoretically for a 'best option' full independence while securing a far more practicable momentum towards a 'federal' UK.

This is because the internal politics and outward presentation of the SNP requires its leaders to leave opaque, for the moment, exactly what their true objectives are. No serious SNP politician sees merit in replicating vastly expensive structures in Scotland where they're not necessary. In fact, most people recognise that ideas such as the creation of a new army, navy and air force is a daft bluff. But, actually, it doesn't matter. It's clear that in pursuing this twin track, the SNP is presently dominating the ground upon which the constitutional future of Scotland, and indeed the UK, will be determined.

After the Storm

Now the dust has settled, the scale and meaning of the SNP's remarkable success in the 2011 Scottish Parliamentary Elections are cast in sharp relief.

The Scottish Parliamentary system was designed to ensure that no single party would have overall control. Ironically, this was in large part to prevent a first past the post electoral method from assuring a permanent Labour advantage which would have lacked international credibility. Now, a mere 12 years after the first elections, there is already a quiet constitutional crisis. The SNP's success has swept away the checks and balances built into the Scottish Parliament. The Scottish Government controls the presidency and has a majority on all select committees; the latter more powerful than their Westminster equivalents, precisely in order to hold the executive to account in a unicameral system.

The Scottish media has been unusually quiet, and largely uncritical, about what would be considered an enormous national problem if it existed at the UK level. This is, at least in part, because while not necessarily in support of SNP policies, the media recognises that the SNP's optimism chimes with their readers however the latter cast their vote.

This whole situation has come about not because of an increase in Scottish public support for classical, 19th Century-style independence, but because most people in Scotland are increasingly confident about both their Scottish identity and the prospects for a largely self-determining nation. The 2007 to 2011 SNP administration did indeed fail to deliver on its key promises, yet the electorate forgave them that in the face of a Labour campaign which seemed unable to see things through a Scottish prism; wholly unable to match the optimism and self-confidence of the SNP campaign with anything other than fear and pessimism.

It is true that the Liberal Democrat collapse was significant to the SNP's success, but the deeper truth is that many naturally left-of-centre Lib Dems, along with more than a few swing voters in Labour heartlands, were heartily fed-up with Labour's negativity. Our electoral strategy was built around an assumption that voters, urged on by a narrative built around the fear of Margaret Thatcher, who left power 20 years ago, would behave the same as they had in the 2010 General Elections. This failure to grasp the Scottish zeitgeist was deservedly disastrous.

And, Coming Right Up?

Some Labour activists argue now that it would be a grave mistake to, as they would see it, allow the SNP to set the agenda in this way. They note, correctly, that the SNP Government in Scotland has mishandled public finances and have made hollow promises which stood no chance of being actualised. For example, the failure to reduce class sizes as promised in the 2007 SNP manifesto has led to unemployment for many of the extra teachers trained in anticipation of the greater number which should have been required.

But because the SNP is essentially following public feeling, rather than policy prescription, they were rewarded handsomely by the electorate year in spite of their manifest failings. For now, the Scottish public mood is informed by the larger picture, and yes, by no little emotion, rather than the detail in which the devil is invariably lurking.

The Scottish educational system is underperforming; there is relatively little public noise about that. Hospital waiting lists are longer and health statistics, especially in Glasgow, are amongst the worst in the developed world. Yet if you go looking for hue and cry, you'll find it tough to find.

In large part, this is because Scottish identity – a sense of difference, even amongst many who have moved here relatively recently – is the dominant prism through which people view their place in the world. But we're to blame too; Labour did too little in power to modernise education, health, policing – Scotland has 32 local authorities and 8 chief constables. We did not create a hunger for change, so the public challenge orthodoxies less and accept outmoded models more. When Labour was in power in the UK, we failed to lay out why Scotland should have different solutions and even under a Tory government we failed to find our political zest. That we find it now is not only critical to Labour's future success in Scotland, but also the UK.

I sense a frustration about Scotland amongst some Labour members in other parts of the UK. 'If they want to go their own way, well let them – they'll be sorry.' And yet that is essentially a Conservative sentiment. A UK without Scotland would be a Tory nation. Some also point out that greater devolution would lead to a review of the voting powers of Scottish MPs. And so it should. As long as Scotland is affected by virtually all legislation, 'devolved' and otherwise, which goes through Westminster, then of course MPs should vote on the first and last stages. But it does seem indefensible that we vote on the detail of, say, schools policy. The quid pro quo for greater devolution would surely require Scottish MPs to abstain from the middle stages of such legislation. This would help secure, rather than inhibit, Labour's ability to win across the UK in future.

I've noted too, some of the Labour Party's great and good lauding the work of the SNP but, with horrible naivety, missing the point that the Tories are artificially weak in Scotland precisely because they have been supplanted by the SNP as the party of the centre-right. For example, the SNP wants to repatriate corporation tax in order to cut it, and therefore cut pubic expenditure in ways which favour the better-off. In the same way as the Tories are seeking to take advantage of the present economic climate to shrink the UK state, the SNP is seeking to present 'London cuts' to do exactly the same. Yet, at present, Labour has no credible reply.

In responding to this crisis, organisation is important. A Scot, Ian McNicol, is the new General Secretary. Another Scot, Charles Allen, is reviewing the way the party works; so there will be no excuse if we miss the essentials. New party structures must reflect the need for us to reflect the prevailing mood of Scottish confidence. We must have, for example, a leader in Scotland. Without that, no-one will listen to us on Scottish matters.

But with greater powers, the Scottish Labour Party will need to hold our own end up. Donald Dewar's achievements were worthy indeed, but his assumptions, 'devolution, yes, but don't scare the horses', look antiquated now. Scottish Labour needs to grow up, find its fighting spirit again and accept the accompanying risk.

For example, are free prescriptions and an absence of tuition fees really progressive? Of course not; they're popular for the moment, especially amongst the better-off, but they have to be paid for by spending less on those who need it most. So Labour needs to attack conservative orthodoxies, to disrupt quiet consensus. To show people, through the force of our own argument and our ability to empathise with the Scottish public, that the SNP way, a right-of-centre way, doesn't fit Scotland at all. If we press home our case with confidence and imagination, people will get it all right. But it won't be easy.

What matters now for Labour is not that we obsessively deconstruct the tactical reasons for our defeat, but instead that we win the battle for hearts; minds will follow intelligent and brave policy alternatives. We must present a wider and deeper philosophy which reflects how people living in Scotland see the world. Most people want mutually beneficial relationships with the rest of the UK and with Europe but they are very firmly Scottish first, and optimistically Scottish at that. They know that Scotland could stand alone entirely separate from the UK but, rightly I think, suspect that we would be the poorer for it. Labour therefore needs to present a vision for a self-determining Scotland which stresses the things Scots value most. Their wallets, for sure, but also strong and effective public services and an emphasis on helping the least well-off to improve the quality of their lives. We need a true, bold, centre-left response to the tacit Tartan Toryism of the SNP.

Crucially, Labour must move on to the Scottish 'autonomy' ground and disrupt the SNP's ability to be all things to all people. This will inevitably force to the SNP to make a more strenuous defence of outright independence in the coming years.

Labour's first leader in Scotland will have a stronger mandate than her or his predecessors as leader in the Scottish Parliament. We have plenty of people with the ability and experience to capitalise on that and to lead strongly, with a sense of purpose. But s/he will also have to learn from the experiences of 'lost leaders', such as Jack McConnell and Wendy Alexander who together epitomised the traits of guile, toughness and original thinking we need at this very moment.

Both of these first-rate politicians suffered from serving in a Labour Party which, institutionally, had rested on its laurels in Scotland for too long. They longed for more freedom but were not bequeathed the time to exercise it. If we can't have them back, and maybe we can, then at the very least their instincts must inform every part of our new agenda.

With a confident vision for Scotland based upon how people's lives can be improved by greater autonomy, Labour can show how the SNP is, by definition, a party which must put constitutional issues before human ones; a centre-right party which appeals to the heart but whose prescriptions appeal mainly to the better-off. But that means we have to appeal to the heart too. Any vision which does not take account of the richness, strengths and confidence of Scottish society, even at the risk of occasional conflict within the wider Labour Party, will fail. And let's not fail.

Richard Robinson

Labour's Good Society and Strong Communities

Richard Robinson is a Labour Councillor in Broxtowe, Notting-ham, where he has Cabinet portfolio for Arts Culture and Leisure. He is also Head of Policy and Business Development at yesMinister. His previous roles include working as Regional Organiser for Ed Miliband's Labour Leadership Campaign in the East Midlands.

There's really no shortage of advice for the Labour Party in the wake of the 2010 general election defeat as it searches its soul. Searching its soul indeed for a vision, narrative and practical policy agenda that will first sustain it between the maelstrom, tedium and emasculation in opposition. And second, serve to metamorphose the way the party connects and sustains a conversation and momentum with the public, now and when back in government.

Some like Alice Miles, look at specific policy issues in trying to determine 'the challenge for Labour'. She refers to the local election results in May this year when the public failed to reject the Conservatives' agenda of punitive spending cuts. She states that "this is the latest evidence that voters have reached a limit in how much they are prepared to continue to fund a universal system of public welfare at ever-increasing cost, which demands nothing from recipients in return, and with diminishingly obviously benefit in terms of social outcomes. *This is the challenge confronting a Labour Party trying to find an agenda for the 21st century".*[11]

Cue a signal to unleash Rowan Williams, the Archbishop of Canterbury in June 2011 who lamented how "the political debate in the UK at the moment feels pretty stuck".[12] His sermon to Labour also contained a stark warning "we are still waiting for a full and robust account of what the left would do differently and what a left-inspired version of localism might look like".

Others inside the party simply ask for a listening ear, and according to Anthony Parker "despite the influx of young members into the party and despite the importance attached by our leader to the new generation, one question still occupies my thoughts, when will our ideas be asked for?"[13]

For the Labour leader though, Mehdi Hasan notes how Ed Miliband has articulated "three distinct challenges to which the next Labour government must be the answer: tackling generational decline where there are fewer opportunities for young people; *strengthening communities* and historical institutions, and reducing the new inequality between the squeezed middle and a wealthy elite".[14]

On strengthening communities, this is again seized upon by Miliband when he states "going forward, we need to rediscover the tradition of Labour as a *grassroots community* movement – not for the sake of nostalgia for the past, but to strengthen our party's capacity to bring about a real change in people's lives".[15]

It will then be my strong contention in this essay that indeed not just the notion of strong communities, but its practical out-workings combined with a coherent and definitive narrative of what a "Good Society" is, can help transform the fortunes of the Labour Party, and facilitate the real generational change in people's lives we yearn and strive for.

Integral to my argument, as well, is that Labour must rediscover its Christian Socialist principles and values. If, as David Landrum has argued, "the Bible speaks to politics because God is interested in government",[16] surely Labour needs to end a 50 year plus hostility and ignorance of its Christian heritage? For example Alastair Campbell's famous quote "we don't do God".

In summary then a powerful triumvirate of Christian Socialist Values, a good society and strong communities will be the cogent vanguard of a resurgent Labour Party and Movement.

Why community?

Enough ink has already been spilt debating the ongoing historical arguments and conflicts over Labour's purpose, meaning and value. Well before the general election defeat in May 2010 where Labour suffered its worst election result since 1918 (bar 1983), and having lost five million voters during a thirteen year span in office, a deep seated malaise had engulfed the party. Back in 2009, Richard Reeves had signalled that Labour was falling, broken and on its knees with no defining positions on the role of market, the purpose of the state, the relationship between individual and social needs, to name but a few.[17]

To further compound the Party's grief and rub salt into gaping wounds David Marquand miserably opined "it is hard to see why anyone outside the narcissistic ranks of the Labour Party should waste mental or emotional energy worrying about its current state or future prospects. There is no mystery about the disease that is now killing it. Under Blair, it made a Faustian pact, not just with one devil but with two; neo-liberalism in economics, and charismatic populism in politics".[18]

Yet ironically enough it was under the same Blair hegemony that the term 'community' spread its tentacles across the UK political discourse. In particular it was noted how "Community workers have always been concerned with the ideological power of the concept of community. We acknowledge its potential to organise oppressed people for collective action and social change. So, with the emergence of Tony Blair and New Labour in the mid 1990s it came as no real surprise that they were quick to spot its inherent power. In his early speeches, Blair spoke repeatedly about the need to renew community to counter the growing fragmentation of life at local, national and even global levels".[19]

So what is it specifically about "strong community" that would so assist Labour's salvation and offer a signpost for a new generation? Certainly one salient argument is that in practical policy terms it significantly allows the party to play to its strengths. We also need to acknowledge an underlying problem; encouraging people to listen when there is still an unfavourable association with Tony Blair and New Labour. So a key challenge therefore is to be identified with something 'fundamentally different'.

Perhaps the way forward is more obvious than first realised. A huge reservoir and enrichment that Labour should utilise and dwell upon in order to build strong communities is to renew its marriage vows with the co-operative movement. Co-operatives are based on the values of self-help, self-responsibility, democracy, equality, equity and solidarity. In the tradition of their founders, co-operative members believe in the ethical values of honesty, openness, social responsibility and caring for others.

Some have argued however that during the Thatcher onslaught the co-operative movement was effectively destroyed in the 1980s, and what remains is being propelled by a neo-liberal tidal wave. This argument has been powerfully rebutted by Kieron Merrett as he contends "we are strongest when we focus on how co-operatives do better for people than private enterprises, putting people before profits. That is why the Labour left should embrace the co-operative movement wholeheartedly".[20]

Crucially Merrett also highlights how the very message and values of the co-operative movement also allows a clear dividing line and distinction to be made from a Tory Party determined to shrink the state, whilst at the same time proclaiming salvation in the amorphous Big Society ideal.

'It's the community stupid' – some practical examples

Turning to what "strong community" might actually look like in practice I draw upon empirical evidence from my experience as a Labour and Co-operative councillor. We should not cease to remind ourselves though, that whatever level we represent the Labour Party, as branch member, councillor, MP or MEP we realise all too well just how much the odds can be stacked against us. Not just the rantings of the right wing press that seek to slay us, but as Oscar Wilde so rightly stated 'Socialism's great, but it takes too many evenings'. It's hard and takes hours of hard slog often behind the scenes unnoticed, as we seek to change society, driven often by the vision of the public good, whether as a school governor, faithful attendee of the local branch meeting, manning the street stall or delivering the leaflets in the rain.

Whilst of course there are notable exceptions in the country, by and large the Tory way is easier and different. No such lingering desire to be involved, to get stuck into those grassroots issues – it's real lassaiz-faire, exemplified perfectly by Nicholas Ridley during the Thatcher hegemony when he proclaimed 'local councils should meet just once a year to hand out contracts'. One might well ask the Prime Minister how this notion fits in with his 'Big Society'.

But what does a 'strong community' look like? I would like to expand how, in my own council ward in Broxtowe (Kimberley and Cossall), community initiatives have been successfully built (in particular between 2007 and 2011), campaigns run with people empowered, leading in turn to much better results for Labour. I am not for one minute saying I have the monopoly on ideas, I know up and down the country there are many instances where Labour councillors are getting their hands dirty, toiling away – often behind the scenes to build a better society. I refer to my own experience simply as I can see initially where I got things wrong, and then more importantly how, through changing the approach and vigorous campaigning, showing that, in the end, it does actually serve to make a real difference.

I've been a Labour councillor in Broxtowe, Nottingham since 1991. I've never enjoyed the luxury of a 'safe seat' and in the May 2007 local elections whilst I retained my seat, the other two seats in the three member ward went to the Tories and Lib Dems respectively.

I recall Lord David Triesman when he was General Secretary of the Labour Party (and before he was ennobled) saying how Labour infamously lost the Brent East parliamentary by-election on 18 June 2003 because 'we had lost our ability to campaign'. This thought remained constantly with me.

In 2007 I'd probably become a little complacent and perhaps taken voters in my communities a little for granted. To correct this, in the following four year spell between May 2007 and May this year what I can only describe as an avalanche of campaigning ensued in my council ward.

I might here emphasise the significance of 'community' is not just reflected in Labour's ability to campaign at grassroots levels. It's very much about the quality of people's relationships and environments, their 'social capital', their sense of tradition, place and reciprocity.

There's a central lesson too stemming from community organising in that it's essential to build enduring networks around a vision of the common good, bound together by a solidarity and purpose. A stiff challenge we face against the materialistic mindset of the masses, but nevertheless we should not demur.

What I would say is that a strong community is one where there is a strong "campaigning" activism! Remember as well that it wasn't for nothing that Thomas O'Neill, Sr affirmed *all politics is local.*

Labour will win again where we are strong, and we can be strong when we successfully work with and empower our local communities to thrive. We need to build the power of civil society to achieve the common good, and to the extent that Labour shares that goal, it will surely benefit.

What is a Good Society?

In recent history there's probably no better place to start than The Compass publication in 2006 entitled *The Good Society* which discusses some critical challenges for the left including how Labour develops progressive policies on health, crime and punishment, work life balance, race, immigration and so on.[21]

There's little doubt as the contributors to *The Good Society* spell out that the good society is not defined by acquisition or through material prosperity, neither of which has led to personal fulfilment or satisfaction. They do though delineate a path within our capabilities showing just how society can be renewed through the interaction of the democratic impulse for freedom, equality and solidarity.

At this juncture it is certainly appropriate to disabuse any sort of notion that the 'Big Society' can equate in any way to the good society. Whilst admittedly Jonathan Chaplin has identified that the 'Big Society' is far from being just a slogan and has developed a cogent powerful institutional driver right at the heart of the Coalition government in the form of the Office for Civil Society, he has at same time highlighted how four distinctive 'Big Society' policy goals which include *administrative decentralization* immediately serve to attract criticism, the 'Big Society' being nothing more than pure privatisation with the goal of shrinking the state.[22]

Yet in a timely intervention from Maurice Glasman he warns that as social democracy has become neither social nor democratic, this has in turn, led to Labour deserting this land, with the vacuum now being filled by the 'Big Society'.

Nevertheless Glasman is equally adamant about what the response should be and proclaims "Labour needs to develop the idea of a Good Society as its rival, and such a society would be built on relationships built on *reciprocity, mutuality* and *solidarity*, all the way up and all the way down, in politics and within the economy".[23]

Just what a society embracing reciprocity, mutuality and solidarity might truly look like, encapsulating freedom and equality is clearly not going to be captured within the parameters of one chapter in this book. I find it incredibly difficult though to distance myself from Glasman's compelling vision and analysis of where we need to be. How we get there I suggest, brings me to my last argument, which whilst I accept may not prove universally popular is nonetheless an absolute non-negotiable for Labour's success – it must rediscover its relationship with God.

Where does God fit into the Good Society and strong communities?

Abraham Lincoln once said, *'my concern is not whether God is on our side; my greatest concern is to be on God's side'*. When we are genuinely concerned about the rights and welfare of all people, regardless of their race, ethnicity, class, gender, sexual orientation, religious affiliation, ability, or age – then it's hard to argue we are not on God's side. Socialists fight for these rights.

However awkward and uncomfortable it may be today for large swathes of the Labour Movement to embrace and acknowledge a specifically Christian identity, Paul Bickley has reminded us of an unmistakable "historical taxonomy of the key connections between Christianity and the Labour Movement",[24] Furthermore James Green has asked a very straightforward question "we don't do God, but should we?"[25]

Jon Cruddas then identifies "the problem with Labour is that it used to be religious and civic and it's now secular and statist – and I think there's something to that. Labour at its best was pluralistic. You had different classes, different faith traditions, different philosophical traditions, and the policy programmes were the resolution or the reckoning of those different traditions. Now you have a hollowed-out party which is about retaining power. There's no policy architecture or infrastructure to provide a reckoning from different groups within it. We need to return to our history, in terms of rebuilding that pluralism, rebuilding space where different traditions can rebuild and articulate their different propositions, and these can be resolved and respected in a tolerant manner, and a different policy agenda can be developed accordingly".[26]

Whilst we know the Tories will always claim Christ as their own, as a moderate Muslim, Mehdi Hasan has unswervingly responded how "in word and deed, the son of God was much more left-wing than the religious right likes to believe".[27] Undeterred Hasan is emphatic "Love your enemies. Renounce your wealth. Pay your taxes. Help the poor. Cure the ill (for free). These are the hallmarks of left-wing, socialist politics. What Jesus wouldn't do is allow the rich to get richer, give a free pass to the bonus-hungry bankers and invade one foreign country after another. It is difficult to disagree with Wallis when he says: "The politics of Jesus is a problem for the religious right".

To conclude, it's hardly a secret that the financial crash and the deficit that it generated is the focal point for the political background for the foreseeable future, and certainly at the next General Election.

The title of this book and the ideas contained in it are however designed to propel us to a higher plane, to renew and refresh ourselves in opposition, ready to lift the Labour movement to an apogee. A 'Good Society' and strong communities must be at its very core.

There then seems to me to be an extricable and interwoven link between a re-awakening and sense of an awareness of a living relationship with God and the benign implications for society.

The Peterson translation of Isaiah 58 reads "If you get rid of unfair practices, quit blaming victims, if you are generous with the hungry and start giving yourselves to the down-and-out your shadowed lives will be bathed in sunlight. You'll use the old rubble of past lives to build anew, rebuild the foundations from out of your past. You'll be known as those who can fix anything, restore the old ruins, rebuild and renovate, make the *community liveable again*".[28]

Let's do God, society and community once again.

The Challenge for Education, Social Mobility and Young People

The Rt Hon Lord Knight of Weymouth
What Chance an Enabling State?

Jim Knight was the longest serving Schools Minister in the last Labour Government; he served as Rural Affairs Minister and Employment Minister. He attended weekly Cabinet in the year running up to the 2010 General Election, and was made a Life Peer in the Dissolution Honours List 2010. Jim is now the opposition spokesperson on DEFRA matters in the House of Lords, and also works as a consultant specialising in the use of technology in education and employment.

All political parties will say they believe in giving everyone an equal chance. All politicians will say that they believe in removing the barriers that hold people back, and that they deplore the outcomes showing how little social mobility is improving. What defines us is not our rhetoric but our first priorities in office and then the values in our thinking in opposition.

In office, the Labour Government did some important things, and we should never allow our record on social policy to be dismissed. We did lift half a million children out of poverty; the implementation of the principles of Every Child Matters has a lasting effect. In particular, introducing universal early years provision for the first time will in time prove to be profound in terms of social mobility. What ever else we do in future must include a commitment to universal early years provision with integrated parental support.

So, how ever much the electorate needs to hear us being frank about our failings, we must never cede the ground of having been a great government for children, especially poorer children.

But to move forward we also need to be self critical about the past.

Labour's Record

The existing paradigm of how a schools system should work was driven as hard as it could be. The results were mixed.

If the success of education is measured by exam results it was very successful. England's education paradigm has not fundamentally changed for sixty years. We threw everything at it over the 13 years – money, facilities and many more professionals – and it has delivered what it was designed for. More children leaving school better qualified and going to university, including more children from poorer homes going to university than ever before. We secured the first significant increase in reading scores for 11 year olds for 30 years. The numbers getting at least five higher level grades at GCSE have gone from 36% to 50%. The numbers going to higher education have gone from 44,000 to almost 300,000, despite the introduction of tuition fees.

However, if we measure success in other ways, the system has not delivered for a significant minority of children. We should not allow Gove to define this failing by numbers going to Oxbridge, because there are better measures, relevant for the majority.

Truancy rates are largely unchanged. For the last fifteen years the numbers of 16-18 year olds not in education, employment or training has remained stuck at just over 10%. And most damning of all for a Labour Government; the achievement gap between rich and poor has barely narrowed. The gap at GCSE between Free School Meals (FSM) pupils and non-FSM is still over 25%. If we judge the success of our education system on whether it helps deliver social mobility, then the performance has been disappointing. It has therefore been at the heart of the Coalition's critique of their inheritance that we "failed" on social mobility.

So what is their response?

Our Likely Inheritance

The Coalition has published a social mobility strategy that is little more than a commitment to monitor the situation. Their cross-government actions suggest they believe that the State is part of the problem, holding people back through bureaucracy and dependency. The Big Society is their answer for the most disadvantaged. It supposes that our common sense of decency and community will motivate us to help each other out and re-discover philanthropy, so that third sector organisations help those least able to help themselves. This is, at best, naive and is certainly undermined by the actions of George Osborne in the Treasury.

If you use a life cycle approach to look at those actions it is shocking.

The attack starts before the child is even born with the cut in the Health in Pregnancy Grant. Then life begins and we find the baby credit element of tax credits gone. The Sure Start Maternity Grant has been cut for a significant number of women, and the childcare element of tax credits, and child benefit, are gone from a growing number of middle income families as thousands more move into the top rate of tax. A brazen attack on aspiration and the social mobility of middle income families wanting to continue to climb the strata of society.

Let us then hope the child's family doesn't live in private rented housing, especially in London. Shelter estimates that housing benefit changes will force 129,000 children to have to move to more affordable homes with, as the government's own impact assessment says, "an adverse impact on work to reduce child poverty and children's schooling could also be affected."

Before they get to school, the parents and child might be lucky enough to get support from one of the remaining Sure Start Children's Centres. Much has been made of 15 hours of free pre-school support for some two year olds and all three and four year olds, but where will they go for this support if early years provision is closing?

Then we get to school.

The concept of the new pupil premium is welcome but the reality is that, as the Institute for Fiscal Studies has said, schools in more deprived areas will receive a smaller pupil premium than similarly deprived schools in more affluent areas. In order to pay for it the two most successful schemes that academics tell us narrowed attainment gaps between rich and poor, London Challenge and Extended Schools, have been scrapped or allowed to whither on the vine.

Worst of all is if the child is not academic, he or she will be written off, and turned off school, with the introduction of the English Bac that exclusively values academic achievement and incentivises schools to narrow their focus away from the alternatives of creative and practical learning that may unlock the disengaged. And as the admissions code is weakened there is no protection from schools choosing pupils rather than parents choosing schools. In the free market school system being fashioned by Gove this is particularly dangerous for social mobility.

If the child is not too disengaged by the narrower focus of school, will she stay on after 16? 600,000 students will no longer qualify for financial support who would have received the Educational Maintenance Allowance, even with the new replacement scheme.

If they manage to stay on, what about university?

Most universities are trebling fees. Despite warnings, the Government can't afford this and look set to reduce the number of student places accordingly. What does that do for social mobility?

On any rounded analysis Labour will inherit a deteriorating position on social mobility. So what should be done in education and skills to improve things for everyone, to maximise the advantage to the economy and most important to address social mobility?

Our Future Direction

Parents

All of the evidence says that the secret to a great school is leadership. Similarly, it is well documented that the root of learning in the classroom is great teaching. But we often ignore the fact that the biggest single determinant of the success of a child is the quality of parenting, particularly their involvement in the child's learning.

Too often this translates into an obsessive focus on choosing the 'right school', rather than a good diet, reading a bedtime story, helping with maths homework and equally celebrating achievement in sport, the arts, craftwork and academic results.

This underpins the importance of Sure Start, of integrated commissioning of children's services, of early identification and intervention where there are problems. This necessitates a rediscovery of Labour's enthusiasm for local government and more aggressive internal drivers to ensure quality in councils. I would also be looking at how well payment by results is working in welfare to work, to see whether similar methods can be used to invest now against future savings against the welfare, health, criminal justice and social services budgets. Family intervention projects were expensive but can potentially save millions and we have to create the incentives for these techniques to grow through new invest to save forms of funding.

In schools, we must move on from structures to a drive for standards for every child.

We will inherit an unregulated market in schools. The cornucopia of choice of schools will need addressing but I hope without imposing yet another massive structural change. Some of the new free schools and academies will be successful and popular in communities, and it will be as politically difficult to close these as it has been to end the abomination of grammar schools.

The starting point will instead be the inevitable failure of some free schools, academies, faith schools and the few remaining community schools. With 23,000 schools it is impossible to believe that we will have 23,000 great leaders supported by 23,000 effective governing bodies making every local school a good school.

School Leaders

We must build on the success of our foundation of the National College for School Leadership and the National Professional Qualification for Headship. Continued school autonomy is essential but with better governance, fair admissions and local accountability.

I would want to achieve this through all schools having to be part of a cluster of around 12-15 schools, with an executive head and a single semi-professional governing body. Each school would have a head of teaching and learning, and a school council of parents, pupils and staff to sustain strong school communities. The cluster would act as a mini-education authority with primary, secondary and special schools, with procurement savings, professional expertise and some parental and local authority representation on a board of around a dozen governors led by a paid chair selected on the basis of competence.

This cluster based approach would apply the international experience that the best school systems embrace both autonomy and collaboration, against strong accountability.

The accountability must move on from schools being defined by a snapshot of test scores.

I am attracted by the system I saw in Alberta, where schools were measured in a range of ways including results, attendance, and satisfaction. The school scorecards were then aggregated at a district level and even aggregated again at a provincial government level. If the government showed red on one of their ratings they were required to produce an action plan for approval by parliament. In England, we can build our own version but retain the notion of the same measures for schools, clusters of schools and ultimately the government.

I am also interested in a measure of outcomes. The development of the Universal Credit by the Department of Work and Pensions will make it possible to easily measure the destination of learners one year on from leaving secondary school. The pupil premium is a payment based on input. We should examine the practicality of replacing this with a payment based on outcome as a way of tackling NEETs and motivating schools to finally take careers education and work related learning seriously. If schools get a premium payment if their alumni are still in work or education twelve months after leaving them, we can drive a continuation of pastoral care that can only help the young adult and link better with other young people's services. Then, beyond parents and school leaders, we must also focus on the final element of the trinity of good education: teachers.

Teachers

From Ofsted to even Michael Gove we all agree we have the best generation of new teachers we have ever had. We now know how to recruit teachers. We may have to refit successful systems damaged by Gove's abolition of the Training and Development Agency, the General Teaching Council for England, and the School Support Staff Negotiating Body and his undermining of the pay review body, but we should now focus on what is taught and when it is taught, so that every child is engaged by school. The key to education's contribution to social mobility has to be whether it has something to offer everyone.

Not every child is left brained. Not all of us are stimulated by academic styles of learning, of sitting still and listening, absorbing, reflecting and communicating. Others prefer to learn by doing, by being active, by creating, by interacting. The English Baccalaureate will turn off these children and we need a different driver for teachers to ensure that the tools of technology, of the arts, of work related learning and of sport are used to engage all pupils. We will need an alternative qualifications wrapper that includes a better balance between different achievements in school.

We also need to ensure momentum through school for every child, not just proceeding at the pace of the majority or the whole class. I would advocate three changes to provide this. First, schools should be freer to allow children to proceed by stage not age. As clusters allow the development of more all through schooling this becomes easier, and a more diverse curriculum also means that this will be different for children in different subjects – few of us are genuine all rounders academically, physically, creatively and expressively and so grouping by general ability of age is hard to justify.

The second measure is to end the National Curriculum at 14. This means GCSEs at 14, but fewer of them. It means that the first three years of secondary will be more important which in turn will require a stronger relationship with the last years of primary. Post 14 students will then start to specialise, and may go to colleges or other schools for some of their learning. This will need an urgent renewal of information advice, and guidance in schools and a more consistent involvement by employers with education.

Finally, there is a case for shortening the 14-19 phase by a year. Freed from the break at 16 this is more possible and allows two options. One would be to invest the savings in higher education to fund a reduction in student fees. The other would be to have a transitional year at the end of school that would result in a foundation diploma or an apprenticeship. The apprenticeship option would suit those wanting to either progress to work or have a grounding in practical skills to inform university learning in subjects such as Engineering.

The new diploma would be developed with exam boards by universities as extended projects to develop the independent research skills needed in university, plus some community volunteering work similar to that in the International Baccalaureate. It would be delivered from schools and colleges to allow students to develop from home. The diploma would allow universities to shorten the length of most degree courses where the first year is simply designed to develop research based skills. This in turn would cut the cost of higher education to students.

Conclusion

As a Labour Party our education policies should be measured against their success in tackling social mobility. In turn we should measure social mobility less on entry to elite universities and professions, but more on whether everyone leaves school working and/or learning and that education more closly matches the needs of the labour market. These ideas are a start. Parents first; then accountable collaborative schools; a balanced curriculum; and more affordable higher education along side valuable skills training valued by employers.

Aaron Porter

Where Next for Labour's Higher Education Policy?

Aaron Porter is a higher education consultant and freelance journalist. He served as President of the National Union of Students between June 2010 and June 2011.

When political commentators look back at the Labour government's record on higher education, the vast majority will look to the introduction of £1000 upfront tuition fees by the then Education Secretary David Blunkett soon after coming into government in 1997. Or the politically contentious £3000 top-up fee which was introduced in 2006, which only sneaked through Parliament by just 5 votes and saw scores of backbench Labour MPs rebel against the Government. Up until that point, the vote on tuition fees in 2004 was the closest vote the landslide Blair government had faced, such was the scale of opposition. But an obsession about tuition fees, whilst to a point understandable, obscures a series of serious achievements that the Labour Party should be proud of across higher education more generally and needs to be the basis for Labour's future higher education policy.

Unlike the recent funding reforms from the Coalition

Government to treble tuition fees to a maximum of £9000 a year, accompanied by a £3bn cut (which equates to 80%) of the university teaching budget, the introduction and then increase of tuition fees under Labour was largely additional money which saw English universities enjoy a decade of unprecedented funding. Against a backdrop of two decades of year on year cuts to the higher education budget by the Thatcher and Major governments, this was a deliberate and distinct change of policy from a Labour government, in contrast to its Tory predecessors. It was the first to seriously account for and put money into higher education since the creation of the Open University under Harold Wilson in 1969. The fact that Labour's higher education funding changes brought in extra money to the sector should not be forgotten, and why the current Coalition's proposed changes are so bad for students and universities. It simply shifts the balance of funding from the state to the individual under an incredibly expensive and inefficient system, rather than finding innovative ways to find new revenue streams into our higher education system.

Whilst I am quick to draw attention to differences between Labour and the current Coalition's record on higher education funding, there are a number of striking similarities too. Most obviously, is the consistent failure from both to find a way to bring in a structured contribution from business to help fund the sector. When the former Chief Executive of BP, Lord Browne of Madingley was appointed by Lord Mandelson just before the 2010 general election to oversee an independent review into the future funding of higher education, any remote possibility of funding a structured business contribution was finally extinguished. But given the enormous benefit that business receives from highly educated graduates, the fantastic record of research in UK institutions and the importance of a thriving tertiary education sector to set the right conditions for business prosperity it only seems right that they should make a small, but proportional contribution toward ensuring we can have a well funded university system.

Business will argue that it pays its fair share through Corporation Tax, but given the scale of the cuts to the higher education budget, universities are in receipt of relatively less public funds, a better balance needs to be struck, and Labour would do well to look at a structured business contribution, which takes into account the benefit business obtains from higher education year in, year out. The University and College Union (UCU) have long argued for a Business Tax to fund higher education. They argue that increasing corporation tax to the G7 average would ensure enough money can be raised to abolish student fees completely and adequately fund higher education. Personally, I remain unconvinced that such a blunt approach to funding higher education would lead to other unintended consequences that render the approach counter-productive in the long run, but the broader point that UCU raise which is business should contribute to higher education in a more substantial way is a serious point, which Labour need to address in more detail.

But more fundamental than arguing the relative merits of how higher education should be funded, Labour needs to re-examine the case for why higher education should be funded. As President of the National Union of Students (NUS) at the eye of the storm over the recent debate on HE funding, my biggest criticism of universities themselves was their abject failure to make the case for the protection of funding, and however poorly made was not recognised by government. The relationship between higher education funding and economic growth is well documented and needs to be brought to the fore in the UK again. The Leitch Review of skills, 'Prosperity for all in the global economy – world class skills'[29] (December 2006) made clear that education at all levels was vital in order for the UK to remain internationally competitive, and Lord Sainsbury of Turville in his report 'The race to the top'[30] (October 2007) rightly set out the need for continued investment in HE as well as the need for rates of participation to be increased in education at all levels. Particular challenges are thrown up in relation to overall participation, postgraduate access and our science and technology base which I will address subsequently in my contribution, and need to be important components of Labour's future solution to higher education. But investment in higher education for reasons of social mobility, equality and fairness are vital too, and often neglected component of the debate which appears to have taken a more utilitarian focus in recent years.

Labour's much maligned 50% target was criticised as being dreamt out of thin air, and out of kilter with the needs of the UK economy. I have lost count of the times that I have heard the claim that 'too many people are going to university' but the evidence runs completely contrary to this. Indeed, I will argue that rather than the 50% target being one of Blair's worst policies, I think it was one of his best. It was grounded in sound economics that in order to get 40% of the adult population educated to degree level by 2020, we needed 50% of school leavers to enter higher education. But it isn't just sound economics, it was good for social justice. The expansion of higher education, notably from 1992 onwards has meant that young people from increasingly diverse backgrounds have been able to enjoy the benefits of higher education.

It has been that access to higher education which is able to transform their life chances for a wider range of people than was possible before. The Coalition government's recent social mobility strategy, 'Opening Doors Breaking Barriers'[31] (April 2011) is still able to cite that 'just one in nine of those with parents from low income backgrounds reach the top income quartile', and the ability to get more young people from the lowest income backgrounds into higher education will help us to deliver a more socially mobile society.

Despite a real drive from Labour to get more people from all backgrounds into higher education, we now have around 43% of 18-25 years old going into higher education we have already been overtaken by our international competitors. Since 1998, we have slipped from 3rd to 11th of OECD countries in terms of our school leavers going to university. This means we need to re-double our efforts to ensure that we are opening access to HE for greater and greater numbers of young people.

It is for this reason, if the recent decision to treble tuition fees will seem like an insurmountable barrier for many young people from poor and lower-middle income backgrounds to get into higher education, their decision to strip away the key infrastructure which supported educational progress is probably worse. The last few months have seen the Coalition scrap the Educational Maintenance Allowance (EMA) and replace it with an inadequate and under-funded alternative, and abolish the AimHigher programme which set up vital partnerships between universities and schools and colleges. I believe it is these decisions to end EMA and abolish AimHigher which could have a much more devastating negative impact on access than the increase of tuition fees. But in addition to laying vital foundations to support increased university access like EMA, AimHigher and public support for the 50% target it was raising standards and attainment in schools which gave more and more children the confidence and aspiration to proceed to university. We wait to see whether Michael Gove's recent proposals which include the removal of a statutory duty for schools to provide careers education, and the creation of an English Baccalaureate which places a traditional and narrow focus on educational value, will have anything other than a backward impact on educational retention and progress.

Looking to the future, Labour needs to reassert the value of higher education to the economy and to social mobility. There will be an immediate challenge to see if it can re-invest public funds in university teaching to reverse such an unprecedented cut from the Coalition which has ended the public funding of teaching for all arts, humanities and social science. A future Labour government should re-open a stream of public funding for those subjects as a matter of priority. This should be accompanied with a renewed public backing from government to more people going to university for both economic and fairness reasons.

However, rather than simply focusing on school leavers, I believe that it would make more sense for Labour to talk about the percentage of the workforce population we need to have high level skills, which will begin to address how we start to get those in the 40s and 50s who may have missed the chance to enter higher education when they left school in the 1970s and 1980s to pick up the necessary skills that may be important for them personally, but also to help drive forward the economy. As we look to the future, the idea that one degree studied between 18-21 will be enough to succeed for the workplace in 2050 or 2060 will be outdated. We will need a higher education system which allows adults to enter and re-enter higher education throughout their adult life. This is truly going to be the way in which the UK economy will be able to deliver improved GDP per capita, and a labour market which is able to renew its skill base to meet the needs of a rapidly changing and demanding economy.

Currently, we have a funding system, and public debate about higher education which is largely focused around the school leaver that goes into full-time undergraduate study. But part-time students make up 40% and postgraduates are 20% of the higher education population already, and a responsible Labour Party going forward will now make the case for lifelong learning. One which puts access in and out of higher education and credit accumulation during adult life the centre of its policy going forward. Central to this, it also needs to seriously consider postgraduate funding and access, both of which have been shamefully ignored by successive governments.

The ability to get the brightest and the best British students into postgraduate education is pressing for future economic growth and innovation, but also for reasons of fairness too. We now have as many postgraduate students as a percentage of the adult population, as we did undergraduates in the 1960s and this trend needs to be continued to be supported. However, it is unsustainable under its present form, because there is barely any government support for postgraduate fees, most are left to take out a career development loan, and coupled with soaring undergraduate debts more and more prospective postgraduate students will feel that they can't afford to stay on into postgraduate education and incur yet more debt. This is an issue which can not be ignored for much longer, and we need Labour to address the sustainability of postgraduate education, and crucially find a way for the brightest and the best to stay on in education. Perhaps my previous suggestion of a structured business contribution might actually be best focussed to simply create new routes and funding streams into postgraduate education, as the economic return is likely to be more obvious and immediate.

During the Labour leadership contest, both Ed Miliband and Ed Balls strongly made the case for a graduate tax. As an evolution of the then funding system for full-time undergraduates, and a striking contrast to the Coalition's proposals to treble tuition fees and introduce a variable market in price for undergraduate fees will emerge when the system comes into effect from September 2012, both Miliband and Balls advocated a fairer and more progressive system than the Coalition were prepared to. But given that we will have a market system in force in just over a year, alongside deep cuts to the teaching budget, the transition to a graduate tax will be complex to administer.

The immediate priority for Labour should be to try and restore public funds, to look at a solution for postgraduate funding and access, and to shift higher education policy to look more holistically at lifelong learning and allowing entry and re-entry into a system later in the life. The promotion of work based learning opportunities to ensure we can meet the skills needs of the future, and continuing to ensure higher education is contributing to social mobility for people of all ages and backgrounds, will allow Labour to strike a political advantage against the Liberal Democrats who have let down students, and the Conservatives who have once again retreated to 1980s style deep cuts to the university budget.

Dr Nick Palmer

A Constructive Response

Nick Palmer was Labour MP for Broxtowe from 1997 to 2010; he is currently Director of Policy at the BUAV, one of Britain's leading animal protection campaigns. He has a PhD in mathematics from Birkbeck College, London, and spent 18 years in IT management for a leading multinational company.

Opposition politics has its consolations. Golden Labour Parliamentary moments have to include Harriet Harman noting that Nick Clegg had promised to abolish tuition fees, and sweetly asking him to update the House on his progress. Serious issue though it is, you'd have needed a heart of stone not to laugh.

However, having had fun with the Liberal Democrats, we are at some point going to need to come up with something better, aren't we? The default option is to say that it's very regrettable, but we can't unbreak the egg, so let's all get used to £9,000 – but maybe we'll promise not to increase them again for a bit. That isn't very inspiring. Can we do better? Well, first consider a few preliminary questions.

Do degrees prepare you for work?

The first question is whether we are actually offering useful degrees. I'm not talking about the urban myths of degrees in 'Elvis' and 'surfing', but mainstream degrees which everyone admires. A good few years ago, I did a combined BSc/MSc course, which was the standard where I was living at the time (Denmark). We did five years of mathematics and computing, and felt pretty good about ourselves, until in the final year one of the IT lecturers observed that we shouldn't kid ourselves that we were now actually employable. Sure, we understood programming and signal theory and many other underlying principles of IT, but we weren't really ready for normal commercial work, and we should expect to become trainees until we'd got a year or two actually working with databases and practical user interfaces.

Today, an IT course will certainly include databases and user interfaces, but will it really get you ready for work? This sort of anecdote is dismayingly common – and all too often heard from employers. It isn't that they can't get apparently qualified applicants, but that they have to add a year or two of additional training to help them tackle the actual tasks in hand. The computer games industry (one of Britain's success stories until George Osborne strangled the R&D credit that would have made them competitive with Canada) employs numerous British graduates, but only a handful of universities are seen by the industry as really preparing them for that line of work.

Does this mean that studying is a waste of time? No. Training students to think analytically and critically is important for almost any walk of life except for those requiring uncritical discipline, such as the army or a certain type of backbench MP. But keep in mind the fact that courses and jobs are not really matched closely at the moment. Now, undergraduate degrees often lead on to postgraduate degrees – what about those?

Is postgraduate research useful?

Armed with my MSc, I went on to a PhD in mathematics at Birkbeck College, London. My tutor, the late Professor Dowker, was a leading light in my chosen field of point-set topology, so this was pretty cool. He advised that there were two types of PhD student, both perfectly competent – lions and jackals. Lions would go where no previous student had survived and discover new territory. Jackals would follow the lions and pick up the leftovers that the lions had neglected as they sallied into the unknown. It was, he said, important to decide early on which I wanted to be. Well, of course I wanted to be a lion, but I turned out to be a jackal. My thesis generalised numerous well-known theorems into hypothetical worlds where the normal assumptions of our world no longer existed. How long did it take? Three years. Mathematically, it was impeccable stuff. Practically, it was entirely useless, and I knew as I did it that the probability of anyone finding it remotely interesting was as infinitesimal as the smallest flea on a jackal's bottom. There's a copy in the British Library; if anyone has ever taken it out, I question their sanity. Have I ever used anything in it myself? Hell no. Did it improve my analytical capacity? Yes, probably.

How much did I pay for this education? Nothing. Learning in those days was free. Have taxpayers had value for money? Some, perhaps. But they could probably have got a better bargain.

Now this, like the previous example, can't be entirely generalised. Some PhD work is clearly very useful and relevant to immediate issues. But the lazy assumption that you can't possibly tell what advance in knowledge might lead to something was wrong in this case. It was clear from the very outset that this particular advance in knowledge wasn't going to get anyone anywhere – apart from getting me a better job because my Swiss employer thought the PhD showed I must have a good mind. Might it be possible to get more out of research than that?

Should degrees only be about jobs?

No. I'm really not arguing that the sole purpose of university education is to enable people to go and work for Rolls Royce or Logica or Blizzard. Just that it might be one of the purposes, specifically one of the things that a certain type of student actually wants. And that may be helpful in considering the tuition fee issue.

What is the other way of looking at an employer who whinges that graduates aren't already trained to do the job? It's an employer who is disappointed not to get something for nothing. Why should Rolls Royce expect to acquire someone ready to be productive from day one, without doing anything to help bring that about? I once asked the CEO of my Swiss employer what would make them expand in Britain – he said it wasn't the wage level or the tax level, within reason, but primarily the availability of really good staff. But shouldn't companies be doing more to bring that about?

Perhaps we should stop looking at university education as a single function. With the abolition of polytechnics, we got rid of the overt idea that some universities were closely linked to practical skills rather than academic excellence, but without going back to that sort of class distinction, shouldn't we recognise and welcome the fact that some courses are indeed intended mainly to train people for practical, highly-skilled work?

The Employer Degree Guarantee

What Government could offer would be to bring together universities and employers for specific courses. The deal would be this:

- The employer specifies what sort of training and theoretical background is needed for that line of work and offers input and materials to help.
- The university designs a course (undergraduate or postgraduate), consulting the employer but ensuring that it also includes general training in active, critical thinking. The

employer doesn't design the course – course design is itself a specialised skill – but can reasonably hope that the job needs will be taken into account.

- The employer undertakes to pay a proportion of the student's fees, and to offer successful graduates a guarantee of a one-year fixed contract on leaving, at a normal starting salary for the job.

What's in this for the student? First, obviously, a fee reduction – and given a choice of such offers, the potential to get a really inexpensive course that is nonetheless useful. Second, a definite job offer. There's no compulsion in that, but I've never experienced an economic climate so rosy that students would not welcome a definite prospect. After a year, both the student and the employer can decide if they suit each other – but it's that first job that's often the hardest to get.

What's in it for the employer? The obvious benefit of getting someone who has been training for years for the specific line of work, and the not-so-obvious benefit that the employer will probably be the first choice for talented graduates.

What's in it for the university? The potential to offer an attractive package to students.

What's in it for the Government? Apart from the indirect benefits of having round pegs leaving university for round holes, the reduction of the scale of the issue of student fees and university funding. Because, as we all accept, university education isn't just about jobs.

None of this is actually new. When I first put the thoughts to a constituency newsletter, I was told about a range of deals which universities had done with employers as diverse as nursing and engineering, very much on these lines (though without the job offer). Each of them had invented the wheel by themselves though – a Government-sponsored format linking in to the tuition fee system doesn't yet exist.

Restoring teaching support

The real reason why fees have gone through the roof is that the current government has whipped away most of the subsidy given to universities for teaching. Universities still get research grants, and they get student fees. The third leg of the table, direct government support, has largely disappeared.

Now I don't really see a case for taxpayers in general subsidising the future Rolls Royce engineer. Let Rolls Royce do it. But for those courses which add less directly tangible value, from languages to history to, yes, mathematics, Labour should be looking at restoring some of the support. The easiest way to do that is probably to offer a subsidy of, for instance £2000 to any approved course that charges no more than £8000, so that the student fee does not exceed £6000. We can argue about what 'approved' should cover – despite the tone of much of this chapter, I'd like to cast the net fairly widely, so that there is genuinely a good range of affordable education across the spectrum. But by separating out the courses that employers are willing to support directly, the sums needed will be smaller and the issue more manageable.

Bottom line

The bottom line, then, would be a choice of less expensive degrees in any area on offer and much less expensive degrees with a potential job attached. If we can offer something like that, we will be entitled to laugh at the Liberal Democrat U-turn with more than a short-term snigger, but the conviction that we can afford something better.

Axel Landin

Reclaiming Our Status as the Natural Party of the Young

Axel Landin has been a member of the Labour Party since the age of 15. He served for two years as Leader of Camden Youth Council, and is currently reading Politics at Cambridge University, where he is an elected member of the Student Union Executive.

L abour should always be the natural party of the younger generations. Few of us would dispute that our years in government delivered vast improvements on the jaded and uncaring Conservative regime that preceded them, and young people certainly cannot be excluded from this: record investment in schools, massive expansion in higher education with a target of 50%, the Education Maintenance Allowance, and in the latter years, the now shamefully axed Future Jobs Fund, rate highly among these.

But somehow, in those years, we also lost our way. With the constant preoccupation with Middle England, which Ed Miliband aptly branded the 'New Labour comfort zone', we were not, on the whole, radical enough. Our policies did not speak to school or university students, or to young workers trying to find jobs and places to live in a nigh-on-impenetrable property market. Our first instinct on observing the painful state of affairs which saw almost twice as many students vote Liberal Democrat rather than Labour might be to retort sardonically "thanks, guys". But to lay the blame for such desertion at the feet of students would be to do them a disservice. As a party, we neglected the young as a constituency, and regaining their trust and support is a vital stage of our journey back to power.

This will not be an easy task. Those who promote the advent of new social media networking as the method to win over the young are not only naive, but deeply patronising. The bulk of this task concerns policy appeal. Consistently low turnout among the younger age-groups of voters has led consistent administrations to pursue policies that directly disbenefit our younger generation, uncowed by the potential of the usual disincentive: a backlash from the penalised constituency. As a party, now is the time to abandon this course. Young voters could be key to our next election victory: seats such as Sheffield Hallam, currently the preserve of our errant Deputy Prime Minister, are ours for the taking; the electorate is overwhelmingly comprised of students who will turn to Labour provided that we can offer a coherent alternative that they perceive to be in their interests.

The first policy arena that we must address is that of higher education. We were right to open-fire on the current government for their monstrous hiking of tuition fees to a whopping £9,000 per year. But our humility requires us to note, however depressing it may be, that the report which recommended such a rise was led by New Labour's favourite businessman, former BP chief Lord Browne, and commissioned by Lord Mandelson. Do we really believe a Labour Government, having determined the terms of reference for this review, would then have ripped it up? For many Labour MPs, one small consolation of our general election loss was that it was the Conservatives and not Labour to whom the implementation of such a deeply reactionary move would fall. We lambasted the Liberal Democrats, and rightly so. But were we not turn-coats of a sort ourselves, having promised not to charge for tuition at all in our 1997 winning manifesto?

Ed Miliband was bold and radical in his leadership campaign. He inspired the younger generations with his uncompromising stance against tuition fees. Worryingly, however, when it came to the parliamentary exchanges over the implementation of the Browne review's recommendations, Labour politicians were forthright in their condemnation of the government's proposals but fell short of proposing an alternative. As a party of progressives, charged as the official opposition with holding to account a government intent on destroying all Labour has done in the aim of furthering equality and opportunity, it is incumbent on us to stick to our guns. A graduate tax is the very least we must promise. But really we should go further: for years New Labour afforded education, and particularly higher education, value not in its own right, but on the basis that it promoted employability, and strengthened the British economy with an increasingly skilled workforce in a competitive world market. Accordingly, we should send the bill for increased costs of university tuition that have arisen as a result of increased participation, to the very businesses that reap huge benefits on the back of all those graduates that our universities produce.

It can reasonably be argued, that there is sense in sharing the cost of a university education between the different stakeholders that benefit from it. Principal among these are the student (or potential graduate) who gains social and cultural enrichment in addition to a likelihood of higher earnings throughout his life; businesses, which thrive in a competitive international market on the back of a well-educated, well-trained workforce; and the state, which in a similar way owes its ability to promote itself on the international stage in no small part to the presence of a honed skill-base. This conception, convincing though it is, should not be pursued on the grounds that it runs counter to the important historical principle within our party that holds education to be a right, rather than a privilege. Additionally, taxing business avoids the conundrum of working men and women who have not gone through university subsidising the privileged group that has; and in view of the colossal sums that modern western companies rake in, particularly multi-national conglomerates (which count among their number companies whose annual turnover rivals the GDP of some developing nations), serves as the most effective method to promote redistribution, an end which we in the Labour Party would be loath to disown.

On a separate but related note, the protests that ensued as a result of the proposed changes to our tuition fees regime are more than noteworthy in analysing the infrastructure that underlies Labour's fightback. For too long, commentators of every ilk have used low turnout amongst the younger demographic to support their claim that Britain's youth is apolitical, uninterested and apathetic. This claim is wide of the mark: our younger generation is rather disenfranchised by the de-alignment that they perceive from all the major parties. The protests revealed a constituency that is passionate, aware, and willing to take action to further their political ideals. It was a reawakening of a youthful activism that had not been seen for decades. Up to 50,000 students took to the streets on 10 November 2010, from all over the country and not only from universities but from our schools – where those that will actually feel the pain of the tuition fees hike are to be found. It was extremely heartening to see the willingness to act among our young population when the going really gets tough. The emphasis now, however, must be on how that passion and zeal may be sustained, and transformed from a one-off uprising into an army of the young, always ready to defend our society and the institutions that we value from those who use political means to decimate them.

When every mainstream newspaper with the exception of the

Daily Mirror deserted Labour at the last election, when a Labour Government had endured the greatest financial catastrophe since the Great Depression, coupled with the greatest political scandal in expenses ever seen, when our party was so indebted we had not a single billboard promoting our campaign to counter those artfully airbrushed mugshots of David Cameron; who could possibly have conceived that we could go on to deny the Conservatives an overall majority? But we did so, and we did so largely as a result of brilliant grassroots campaigns at a local level. In my home-turf of London I witnessed this first hand as MPs such as Jon Cruddas in Dagenham, Andy Slaughter in Hammersmith, and most brilliantly Glenda Jackson in Hampstead defied the odds to successfully defend their seats. Young people will always be at the heart of this form of campaigning. No-one is better at scouring endless streets and estates on drizzly mornings, getting out the message. The next task is to take advantage of the unprecedented momentum of student activism, and inspire across the country, a wave of local activism that will deliver a Labour victory at the next general election. This is to be achieved by articulating a programme that those young people really believe is designed to improve their lives. Students, and young people in general, are inherently radical. They want us to be radical too and that is where, for all that we did, we failed after 1997. With such an astounding mandate, we should have revolutionised the role of the state in a positive, proactive way; a real enabler, empowering every citizen. Blair called his public sector reforms radical, certainly, but they were, in fact, the opposite; revealing only a fear to challenge the status quo and appear too...well, Labour. Was it radical to privatise Britain's railways? Not really. It was easy enough to do. But it was nonsensical, even from the perspective of a neo-classical economist. A system with multiple operators competing for customers and thus, from a capitalist perspective, driving prices down and standards up, was understandably impracticable: on almost every route one private company or another has a monopoly and standards, compared to those abroad, are considerably poor. It is a timid, weak politician who identifies the 'middle-ground' and writes a manifesto to echo its perceived wants (which are usually rather the wants of the populist media, now so-discredited). A bold, radical politician takes on the modern phenomenon of the 'populist establishment' as it could be known, and works to persuade the electorate that a radically different doctrine would actually be to their benefit.

Within our party, we need to see Young Labour grow to a new prominence. Whilst Ed Miliband has now delivered on his campaign promise to employ a dedicated staffer for Labour's youth arm, it does not yet have the autonomy that it needs if it is to capture the imagination of the wider young populace, a huge untapped base of potential door-knockers come 2015 or whenever this Faustian Pact government finally exhausts the patience of the Liberal Democrats. Young Labour needs to be a campaigning organisation in two ways: externally promoting our party, recruiting members, spreading the word and organising; but also engaging with our internal policy debates, agreeing clear policy stances that reflect young people's values and interests, and lobbying for their adoption.

As for our young leaders, whilst the precocious type who judges his merits on his ability to parrot verbatim the 'leadership line' may feel at home at drinks receptions in Portcullis House, he will find it harder to inspire the young people of the protests who could form the backbone of Labour's fightback. Real grassroots work and an ability to think for oneself is what distinguishes the exceptional among our party's younger generation. Small initiatives at a local level can have a huge national impact. If every young Labour activist from across the country who attended the protests rang up ten people each that they'd met on Whitehall that winter day and signed them up for party membership, think how much more formidable our campaigning force would be.

There are, of course, many policy areas other than higher education that significantly affect the lives of younger people, and we as a party must review our stances on these accordingly. Recent figures reveal that almost three quarters of young families are unable to get on the housing ladder. The Conservative Government's capping of housing benefit and scrapping of regional housing targets has done little to redress this. Labour needs to advocate a large-scale programme of building social housing for rent, and to expose the disgraceful reclassification of 'affordable' homes as 80% of the market rent. Elsewhere, we should be unequivocal in regarding the marketisation of schooling as an extremely dangerous game to play with something as sacred as our children's primary and secondary education. Whilst academy status may have, in certain cases, greatly improved attainment in previously failing schools, the measures put in place to achieve this (improved facilities, a dynamic head etc) can be applied without removing the school from the sphere of local democratic accountability. Certainly, the collateral damage that academy status entails – requiring schools to compete against one another for admissions in a destructive and divisive manner – outweigh any cited benefits.

It also clouds the real problem facing many schools: private schools drain away local middle class intake from local community schools, which as a result are not properly comprehensive. We should have no truck with any retention of the 'charitable status' that is in effect a £100m subsidy for private schools from the taxpayer. We should go further and require that the number of comprehensive-educated pupils in our top universities is proportionate to those in the wider population (this could be introduced in phases so as not to destabilise the system) which, on the basis that many parents unscrupulously opt for private schools as a queue-jump into better universities, would be more effective than anything thusfar introduced in the objective of an outstanding and fair schooling system for all young people. Admittedly, post-code lotteries would remain an issue affecting how representative of society the make-up of school student bodies are, but at least this is a start. We should have little time for arguments that Middle England would desert us as a result: only 7% of British children are educated in private schools. Accordingly, whilst we may be keen to be perceived as 'on the side of aspiration' for 93% of the electorate this form of aspiration is out of reach, and we insult them whilst we remain silent on this injustice. That those privileged 7% dominate senior positions in society shows how much our country would benefit from radical action to open up our education system.

Young people have the potential to be the driving force behind Labour's return to power. They embody the energy and idealism that a Labour programme necessarily entails. They are not lazy, uncaring and apathetic as we are often led to believe, the last year tells us this much. But for us to benefit from their youthful zeal we must win back the trust of Britain's youth. And this requires us to change: to retain the best elements of our years in government whilst trying to do better where we fell short. We need to recognise that being radical does not mean going further than the Conservatives in reactionary public-sector reforms, it means coming up with our own, better ideas: in other words, to paraphrase the title of Ken Livingstone's well-attended Progressive London Conference last January, 'there is an alternative'. The younger generation will only be inspired by a party they see as really speaking for them in every policy area where they are affected. The key message to heed is that it is policy that is important. Social networking technology will make it far easier for us to get through to young people than ever before, but it will not be the deciding factor in whether we can earn our rightful place as the political home of the young.

A New Approach to Business, Enterprise and the Economy

James Frith

New Ideas for Labour's Fresh Economy

James is the Managing Director of U-Explore and Labour Councillor for Elton, Bury North. U-Explore provide creative digital products and services to Education, Voluntary and Corporate sectors. James was elected in May 2011 defeating the Tory candidate and becoming the first Labour Councillor in Elton for over 10 years.

Governments don't like risk but growth economies need risk takers. So why is the default setting for debate on the needs of business stuck on red tape? Small medium enterprises (SMEs) are not just the engine rooms of any new economy or one needing to grow. They are the nimble footed, responsive and resilient matter, that help protect a stalled economy from falling back into recession and hold the potential to take an economy from good to great. The issues that small businesses face involve cash flow, investment, the cost of recruiting talented people, and getting paid by clients on time. Cash flow problems can put a business under and cause an increase in local unemployment. With over 75% of the UK economy relying on SMEs, the problems they overcome go way further than any government policy to retain people in work, so protecting against greater unemployment.

Small firms on the front line of Britain's emerging industries experience a lack of knowledge and understanding from others about their expertise or industry and the opportunity they present to the challenge of growing our economy. They are misunderstood, ignored or overlooked by those we elect or expect to identify such prospects.

Rather than side stepping the complex factors SMEs face, our policy makers and ministers should demonstrate an improved knowledge of business and a modern view of the small business. Appeasing tired arguments from a minority who continue to pretend employment legislation, seeking a fairer workplace with equal opportunity for all, is hampering their growth or profit-making potential, should cease. This is not an issue, and it has not been for a long time.

Let's give some thought to the policies which may aid the natural growth of these industries and contribute to solving the problems outlined. The focus on smaller organisations is right, as too often in the stretch from small to large size these businesses achieve scale, inject structure and process and this very injection will meter out its impact on that organisation's ability to strike out with new ideas as they once did.

I would like to introduce the concept of thermal economics here, an economic equivalent to what physicists refer to as thermal expansion which can be described as: the general increase in the volume of a material as its temperature is increased. The economies and sectors upon which our future national livelihood depends, are sectors which will expand in direct accordance with the attention they receive – not heat but investment.

Investment is not just money but priority and attention. It is true that the more time spent in research and development (R&D), the greater the prospect, potential and impact of the product or the scope of the industry in question. The problem comes when R&D has to be suspended while these same businesses apply their talent to just staying in business, so suspending the pursuit of what comes next because of what has to be done now.

Concentrating on addressing these circumstances can provide Labour with a renewed vigour and an updated application of a Keynesian approach to supporting business. This approach would help cultivate higher levels of employment, arrive at inventive solutions to modern life and better compete globally if emerging high specification technical, digital industries and manufacturing or green futures sectors get the support they need. These industries of small and micro-sized enterprises are calibrated according to the investment or monies available to them at any given time. A principle of thermal economics is a belief that these sectors will reward high levels of investment with high growth and increasing employment. If we miss this, we perhaps risk overlooking a way out of our stalled economic state. Labour, as Her Majesty's Alternative should take this digital Keynesian view and outline investment plans to help create and sustain these fresh economies for Britain.

Labour must broaden the conversation with business and make the running on this. This is not about getting close to business, but a closer understanding of the daily experience of running a business and the challenges they really face. This is Labour's duty in a bid to build its credible alternative for the UK, for new jobs, new money, fresh ideas and a future economy.

Banks are being encouraged to lend more to businesses. Labour should be telling banks to charge businesses less and stop taking so much of their earnings, thereby assisting with cash flow and letting them grow out of their restricted state. Micro and small businesses rely on cash flow to survive. Very often, valuable business can be on the horizon, items or services sold for the future with invoices raised and payable, but the delay in the arrival of the cash risks seizing up their operation. Invoice discounting is one way a small firm can survive this risk with the factoring of invoices, receiving 80% of the value in advance of cleared funds. The problem with this is that it is an expensive way of earning revenue and restricts growth with the reduced returns on the business made. Can Labour achieve a detailed enough appreciation of this and provide a competitive alternative to invoice discounting provided by the state? This could ensure a modest return for the taxpayer for its support for those businesses' growth and their emergence as large employers in our broader economy. Labour should also commit to granting town halls the right to retain, for reinvestment, the business rates they collect.

Regional Investment Communities (RIC) could combine a social democratic party's commitment to investment for growth, support for independent and private enterprise whilst also restoring power to local communities. RICs are aimed at expanding the identified growth sectors and set up to receive direct capital funding with few conditions for use. This money is divided into risk categories and available to independent, public, private and 3rd sectors. Each of these sectors is free to pitch for the capital with their proposition being presented visually, in theatre and online to the communities they seek commission from. Capital for investment and growth is split into proportions allocated to high, medium and low risk investments. The investments are offered to local communities with all sectors and organisations presenting their ideas to the assembled. Voting would determine progress on investments of all risk levels. The financial returns are set to come back to the local economy. Crowd sourcing and its instinctive caution can provide a discipline with the community sharing the idea, its success and open to its possible failure. The issuing of this capital is done alongside a communication explaining the need for the management of risk and the sharing of the decision-making among the community.

With few formally appointed officers, these communities will be organic and rely on the judgements and collective agreement on projects in those communities they emerge from. The community will not need unanimous decisions but a democratic process can ensure majority. Where highly sensitive or specialist knowledge is required to assist decision making this can be a constitutional matter in the terms by which RICs operate. Communities can have chances to buy in further expertise as part of any commission.

Where the projects commissioned enjoy profitability so the local community benefits with increased investment in local provision or a bonus return for those involved. Statutory duty can help safeguard significant failure or losses. The engagement and decision-making is key with the community gravitating towards the best pitch and one which offers a fine and attractive balance between prosperous returns and security on investment.

Profits from the community investments should be subject to local decision-making as to how these are spent. If Labour wanted to take this further, it could advocate that tax payers should, after a volume of tax paid proportionate to earnings, be able to opt into paper trailed tax codes. As with the example of profits from community investment, this would be an opt-in request that their tax goes on specific capital investments, local work or government sectors. One tax payer may choose research into dementia, another to scientific research or the arts, and a local enterprise within an identified sector for growth.

Labour's record in government from 1997 to 2010 is a proud one in which Britain enjoyed more openness, greater prosperity and fairness. Indeed, at its most radical, Labour prevented a great depression with its swift, clear and precise recapitalising of the banks. Much of Britain's improved settlement enjoyed by many during this period is now at risk by the Tory disassembling underway. A swift return to power for Labour has to be our priority. Reflections on our period of government provide us with opportunity to reframe our proposition whilst we serve in Opposition.

During Labour's period of government, enterprise, aspiration and economic growth were the returns for the early prudence demonstrated in the first term. The government enjoyed the taxes taken from the City's high value financial trading and a booming house market. It oversaw a public and eventually unhealthy culture of large private borrowing against inflated home values to fuel weekend spending in out of town retail parks. This growth in consumption helped economic growth, the en masse purchase of furniture, white goods etc. will always be a key part of any macro economic concern, but the borrowing by government and its citizens was never sustainable. It was an error to suggest boom came without bust, that spending came without a bill and appears to affirm a view that high levels of borrowing, by us all, was sustainable.

Investing in areas outlined previously will help create wealth with new jobs from emerging sectors. Investment in nimble footed, responsive smaller independents can ensure benefits from new technologies or inventive approaches in Labour's continuing commitment to reform in public services. To commission a contract, or simply hand over services to a private sector, as the Tories wish is the wrong approach and will darken much of the improved experiences of public services improved between 1997 and 2010.

I wish to draw on the distinction between a contract and a covenant. Whilst Tory central and local governments line up to privatise public services, Labour should begin with a covenant with the nation. This distinction between the two approaches would provide an approach Labour could apply to its commitment to the provision of public services whilst enabling independent and small provider growth.

The management of a school by a headteacher, to take one such example, can be achieved more effectively with the freedom to choose from a range of market provisions for discretionary or supplementary needs. They can do so on less than the typical 11% surcharge applied to a schools budget with Local Authority control. This should not remove the requirement for the public sector assurances and statutory duties of care provided by an LA. It seeks to counter an unhealthy familiarity or an old order of en masse provision where a monopolistic approach to public services might prevent benefit from cutting edge or the newest products and services. Development of digital technologies, equipment or scientific progress to take three examples emerge traditionally better from independent and smaller sectors in advance of a broader public sector acquiring or adopting them.

Labour should lay out its covenant for public services, setting out enshrined standards it would govern to deliver. This is an advance on the public, private funding models from recent terms of government which demonstrated themselves as effective, though too often far too heavily weighted to the private capital investor. A balanced public and private funding approach provides the healthiest prospect for sustained investment in public services. It is a Labour mind that agrees that towns shouldn't have to wait endlessly for its hospital, new school or walk-in medical centre when such an approach could be taken. With certainty though, these funding arrangements shouldn't, for example, come with a ten year profit making sting in their tail for the tax payer and Labour must lead on these expectations.

Defining Labour's future offer should include ensuring that handsome agreements come with the state's conscience. This includes determining sustainability, limiting profits, demanding reinvestment and focusing hard on competences to deliver minimum service levels as good or better than the entirely public provision preceding it. Labour's covenant must include its unending support for workers and with these thoughts in mind, should extend to a campaign to improve trade union representation in the private sector.

Labour needs to summon a dedicated enthusiasm and a central strategic vision to create new and private sector jobs if it is to offer a counter to the shrinking proportion of private sector employees to public sector levels of employment over recent decades. This will need to be a combination of investment in capital projects and public provision but it must also feature a credible strategy to support new business, start ups, entrepreneurial activity and new economies for the future. It will not be enough to churn the money that exists or simply use government to plug future holes in demand. New money is required from new ideas and a fresh approach to emerging sectors if our own economic credibility is to become an attractive proposition for Britain.

Matt Pitt

The Case for a British Investment Bank

Matthew Pitt is a Parliamentary Researcher who regularly con-
tributes to left foot forward on economic matters and issues af-
fecting young people. Born in Germany, he eventually moved
to England for study purposes and recently graduated from
King's College London.

The current economic situation is undoubtedly bleak with inflation running high, household income falling in real terms, exports growing disappointingly slow despite a weak pound, an extremely low interest rate that has failed to stimulate sufficient business investment and youth unemployment threatening to create a lost generation. Combined with the non-existence of a solid growth plan, it is tempting for Labour to concentrate its fire on a critique of the deflationary impact of the Tory economic theory of expansionary fiscal contraction. But to win in 2015, a positive message of where Labour can help build new capacity in the economy will be a vital element in a credible, pro-growth agenda to generate greater prosperity by 2020.

While it certainly falls to the opposition to rail against Government policies that it deems unfair and regressive, the other side of the coin is to propose what it would do differently by coming up with bold and well-thought through ideas. In March 2010, Hazel Blears highlighted the need for more focus on Labour's economic alternative and quite rightly called for a bolder and more explicit Labour approach. Although it did not get the publicity it deserved, her analysis reflected the pressing question the electorate are posing: how would Labour promote growth, reduce the deficit and bring an end to this nightmare of ongoing economic uncertainty?

It is therefore now, more important than ever, for Labour to begin taking a front seat on the debate and begin answering the most systemic weakness in economic performance under the Coalition. Ultimately, random or unconnected policy ideas will not produce a credible economic manifesto for 2015.

How to Promote Growth and Reduce the Deficit

Disappointing business investment figures across the UK have increasingly led to calls for alternative ways of providing finance for small and medium-sized enterprises (SMEs) and large-scale projects that are failing to access vital funding. With exceptionally low interest rates on public debt and an economy suffering from continued weak demand, the first step Labour should therefore take is to begin advocating a financing mechanism that will meet the markets' investment demands which banks and the stock markets are presently shirking away from. Killing two birds with one stone, such a mechanism – a national investment bank – would not only promote growth in areas that remain relatively stagnant, but also help to reduce the deficit by guaranteeing a safe and profitable return on investments made.

Especially when it comes to extensive projects, private capital markets typically fall prey to seeking out the quickest and most rewarding options and, in consequence, overly neglect sectors such as the green economy. The task to provide finance for such undertakings is one that a publicly-funded investment bank can take by following a list of criteria used for approval purposes that are based on a long-term view of the economy, benefits for society and the fulfilment of carbon emission targets.

Fundamentally, with the idea of a publicly-owned investment bank having not become so alien with the bail-out of RBS, Lloyds and Northern Rock, the current situation presents itself as a perfect opportunity for the Government to take a great stride towards solving the ongoing growth dilemma by boosting aggregate demand through the set-up of a national investment bank. Indeed, the idea of a British Investment Bank (BIB) is not breaking news but was put forward by Peter Mandelson, the former Business Secretary, back in 2010 when he outlined his idea of modelling it on Germany's Kreditanstalt für Wiederaufbau (KfW) that was formed in 1948 with funds from the Marshall Plan. Initially meant to rebuild the country's ravished infrastructure after the Second World War, it quickly became a major lender internationally and domestically, which is highlighted by its recording of EUR 400 billion on its balance sheet in 2009. Fully owned by the federal government and the federal states, it has grown to become the fifth-largest capital market issuer in Europe and now raises around EUR 75 billion in capital markets annually. Other successful models of state-run investment banks are Brazil's National Bank, the Nordic Investment Bank (NIB) in Finland, the European Investment Bank (EIB) and the Development Bank of Japan, all of which have become major players in the global economy.

How to Fund the BIB

Traditionally, public assets are financed through expensive methods of raising private investments, followed by building assets and eventually leasing them to the government – otherwise known as private financed initiatives (PFI). The British Investment Bank would completely turn this process on its head by raising cheap finance, investing in growth-enhancing assets and then leasing or selling them to the private sector. If the Government is serious about reducing the deficit, then the pragmatic long-term view dictates that public investments in sectors that are seeking to expand will yield a steady profit and put the country's balance sheet in a better position to withstand the next inevitable economic downturn.

Similar to the above-mentioned institutions, the BIB would initially be seeded with capital by the government. Thereafter, however, it would have sufficient borrowing powers to enable it to raise cheap finance in the capital markets and channel the money into long-term projects and SMEs, whose return would be greater than the initial upfront outlay by the Government. By becoming major capital issuers in the global markets, the existing state-funded investment banks across the world provide an irrefutable example of how a finance mechanism that was initially set up and run through public finance, quickly develops into a permanent funding unit that is able to attract vast sums of private investment and raise its own finance.

In detail, the bank would be able to use two devices to create the vast funding streams desperately needed in the British economy. One would be similar to that of the KfW and the NIB, which issue bonds to institutional investors at favourable rates via their 'AAA' credit rating due to an implicit government guarantee and access to the state's budget. For that reason, the bank creates funding streams at very competitive rates. The KfW, for example, uses this process to raise approximately 90 per cent of its capital.

The method of getting the finance to those in need is rather simple and straightforward: households, small businesses and community groups initially apply for funding through commercial banks that then forward the requests to the national investment bank. In turn, it then evaluates these according to government criteria and, if approved, refinances the loans at cheap rates. In order to ensure that the final borrower benefits from the lowered rates, the BIB would simply follow KfW's example and implement a legal limit for commercial banks over which they are not allowed to charge. As a result, despite being restricted in the amount charged, the banks are more willing to support financially-starved sectors. This is mainly because the previously unavailable money cannot be put directly onto their balance sheets but needs to be passed on. In addition, projects that seemed too long-term and possibly questionable are now guaranteed to go ahead and be completed due to the involvement of the government.

Most importantly, it is the commercial banks that carry the loan default risk and they therefore add an air of credibility to the process by judging the credit-worthiness of the applicant out of pure self-interest. In consequence, the only real danger for the BIB is an actual default by the particular commercial bank on its loans. In this way, primarily requiring a flood of private investment in SMEs and the green infrastructure, Britain would be able to use a financing mechanism that channels money through commercial banks instead of storing it up. Alternatively, instead of using commercial banks, the BIB should also consider funnelling funds through the newly set-up Local Enterprise Partnerships that have the necessary local and regional knowledge but are struggling because of being utterly underfunded and unable to meet investment demands.

The other device to promote essential funding would be the attraction for private investors to become partners in projects that, due to cheap finance and public investment, are likely to become more profitable and lower-risk as a result. In consequence, this would reduce the incentive for the government of resorting to the private finance initiative (PFI) that has typically provided the private sector with often disproportionate and unending profits without the actual transfer or risk from the public to the private sector.

The EIB provides a good example to signify the extent of the potential private funding opportunities produced via initial public funding. Lord Skidelsky, a proponent for a state-investment bank in the UK, used recent figures to calculate that governments which contributed EUR 50 billion of capital to the bank subsequently raised an additional EUR 420 billion on the capital markets. Instead of crowding out private investment, evidence proves that a BIB would ironically crowd them in and increase the overall level of funding, thereby complementing the money initially invested by the bank.

For the UK, the BIB would focus initially on the green infrastructure and the growth of SMEs, because these are the sectors that are going to become major contributors to the growth of the economy, but are facing a crisis of underfunding. Both areas offer the opportunity for creating tens of thousands of new jobs and helping to diversify the UK away from an over-dependence on the financial sector. And yet there remains little effort by the government to create the right environment for them to receive the necessary funding levels. These issues deserve greater examination in the context of a BIB, especially because they are vital to the economy but are being overly neglected by the government despite the repeated rhetoric on the importance of them to the future of Britain.

The Green Economy

The political discourse on the green economy in recent years has experienced a marked shift away from a luxury to be indulged in if economic prosperity allows it and, instead, has transformed into an opportunity for a vast expansion of jobs and growth in troubled times. Although a structural transition towards a 'green economy' is likely to lead to lesser growth in other parts of the economy, the United Nations Environment Programme's 'Toward A Green Economy' indicates that such a negative impact is likely to be mitigated by investments that "help increase economic activity and employment in the short run". Ultimately, the report states unmistakably that a consistently large investment "will result in the long run, in faster economic growth". It is therefore of utmost importance for Britain to achieve a strong capability in green technologies that will push it towards a world-leading competitive position and help it create jobs, expand exports and encourage substantial private investments.

Disappointingly, the 'Green Investment Bank' (GIB) set up by the Coalition has fallen far short of requirements. Instead of being able to raise finance itself, the 'bank' will now only receive £3 billion in start-up public capital. Its borrowing powers will commence in 2015 under the condition that public debt is falling by then. This policy stands at complete odds with research conducted by the Department for Business, Innovation and Skills that shows Britain's green infrastructure requires approximately £200 billion by 2020 to ensure the country is on the right path towards a low-carbon economy.

Despite such chronic underfunding, Vince Cable, the current Business Secretary, insists that the initial 1.5 per cent of the required amount will "accelerate private-sector investment". In truth, we are still waiting for a detailed plan on how such small start-up capital will lead to the necessary levels of investment. Notwithstanding, it is a first positive step towards forming an independent publicly-funded bank that will concentrate on green infrastructure projects, such as offshore wind, waste and energy efficiency – albeit a very small one when compared to the KfW that provided 14 per cent of global climate finance in 2008.

Correspondingly, Labour should reinforce and expand the argument on the need to create a green national investment bank that has the capability to raise finance in the capital markets immediately and thereby attract vast sums of private investment. It should not, however, leave it at that. It needs to further outline how a BIB would be able to encourage sufficient private investment to reach carbon emission targets and be daring enough to propose greater initial funding.

SMEs

SMEs are the powerhouse of the UK economy, employing about 60 per cent of the country's private workforce and producing an output equivalent to over 33 per cent of GDP. It is from this sector that the next giant firms will spring forth if it is correctly cultivated through easily obtainable and efficient funding opportunities. Unfortunately, as it stands, approximately 99 per cent of SMEs register less than 200 employees and other figures show little reason for optimism, with around a third of them failing three years after being set up.

The need for the economy to diversify away from its over-reliance on the financial sector and towards manufacturing and entrepreneurship has become paramount in light of the catastrophic impact of the credit crunch on the economy, which is expected to lead to a permanent 10 per cent loss in GDP. SMEs in Britain were hit especially hard by the financial crisis that cut off their primary source of capital, despite the previous Labour Government having bailed out the banks and introducing numerous initiatives, such as the Enterprise Finance Guarantee. As it stands, initiatives such as Project Merlin and the Local Enterprise Partnerships are failing to get the required capital to SMEs that find themselves overly neglected by the Government.

The creation of a BIB would be the much-needed lifeline to SMEs that are being starved of necessary finance, despite the hocus-pocus of Project Merlin that committed the banks to lend £76 billion to SMEs in 2011, which represents a 15 per cent increase on 2010 levels. The initiative is failing to get the necessary funding to SMEs because it did not tackle the new lending criteria that are based on a new culture of playing it safe – too safe – and concentrate on storing up capital. This particular sector is likely to face even greater difficulties once borrowing becomes more inaccessible and expensive when the banks are regulated more tightly and are told to increase their capital holdings.

A BIB would therefore be able to offer cheap finance through the underfunded Local Enterprise Partnerships and also the commercial banks that channel funds from the national bank through to SMEs. It could thereby gradually provide the solution to the level of lending to SMEs – an issue that Vince Cable described as a "serious problem" – whilst boosting growth in the economy by providing much-needed finance. An additional side-effect, apart from increased tax returns, would be an improved external balance due to manufacturing being a heavily exporting sector. In the short-run, even a small fiscal commitment would be sufficient to "offset the £87bn of reductions in public investment planned before 2015".

Conclusion

The state-backed investment bank would channel much-needed capital in the range of billions of pounds to the development of the green economy and businesses that are being starved of funds following the credit crunch. In a short space of time, it would begin raising its own finance, provide government-backed bonds in an under-utilised market and bring in sufficient banking expertise for a socially beneficial cause.

Ultimately, the question is not whether public or private investment should be seen as the driver of economic growth, but which one achieves the greatest social benefits, generates revenues and becomes self-financing. A bank using public funds and private capital to secure growth and a continuous revenue stream by making loans and using capital for big, long-term projects and providing for SMEs' needs is a timely idea. Especially when it comes to the greening of our economy, a market that is high-cost and produces returns over a prolonged period of time needs a funding institution that is able to encourage private investment and make significant contributions itself. Similar to the KfW, the bank's operations could eventually be divided into further subsidiaries that focus on specific sectors other than the green economy and SMEs, such as housing, transport infrastructure and international development.

More than likely, Cameron's ideology prevents him from considering the establishment of such a bank. It would, however, be a credible and forward-looking alternative for Ed Miliband to back. Various other publicly-funded investment banks – such as the EIB and the KfW – now pay for themselves and operate in a well-regulated financial system, so why should Britain be lagging behind other countries by not taking a step from a socially useless banking system to a socially useful one? All in all, a BIB presents itself as the solution to reducing the deficit and producing the necessary growth to the economy. In other words, it is the plan B that Labour has been calling for.

Health and the NHS

Irwin Brown

A Socialist Plan for Health

Irwin has extensive experience of working in many NHS or-ganisations in consultancy roles and as an executive and non-executive manager. He is also an occasional advisor to the Labour Health Team. Any opinions in the article are personal and not expressed on behalf of any organisation. The ideas are to stimulate a wider debate on future policy not an evidence-based prescription for the NHS.

The NHS needs to change to meet rising expectations, demographic pressures of an aging population and advances in technology. It is vulnerable to the tremors running through our failed social care system. It needs to adapt a culture based on reacting to illness into one based on actively keeping people well; from cure to prevention; from care in hospitals to care nearer home. It relies too much, and spends too much, on care delivered in institutions, mostly hospitals, and not enough on prevention, community and primary care. We have to break down the institutional and cultural barriers which prevent care being delivered around the needs of patients; and remove the barriers between 'health' and 'social' care.

The founding principles of our NHS make it free at the point of need and that is seldom challenged. That it is also universal, comprehensive and paid for out of general taxation is still fundamental to our view but are no longer quite so certain. But change is necessary and all agree change is difficult.

The way ahead is not through reorganisation of structures or making health care into a regulated market. What is needed to improve the quality and efficiency of the NHS is not, primarily, organisational change, but changes in clinical behaviour. The answers are not found just through competition and innovation through the private sector. We set out the key themes for an alternative which can be achieved through incremental change – not another radical reform. Our views are our own but informed by widespread discussion with clinicians, campaigners, and party members.

Public Health – Prevention and Education

We need to begin our thinking at the point where we could have the greatest impact in the long term, with public health. Clearing the slums, putting in clean water and sewers did a lot for our health, and better road design has reduced mortality as much as better surgery. In recent years the smoking ban was probably the most important single policy as far as effects on health are concerned. People who take enough exercise, eat enough fruit and vegetables, don't smoke, and drink in moderation live on average 14 years longer than people who don't. These are not things over which the NHS has much influence. The pricing and marketing of food, drink, and cigarettes are not susceptible to local action. They need intervention at a national level.

Top down legislation needs to be met by bottom up measures which try to educate or nudge changes. A major shift in thinking is required to put public health professionals into the key places where decisions are taken and to establish the function where it can be most influential.

Responsibility for all of our wellbeing, including health, should be within local authorities so the links to environmental and social issues can be made. Moving responsibility for public health into local government will give elected representatives the opportunity to make a real difference to the health of their communities.

Active Care – Involvement

Involving people in their own health has a beneficial effect. The NHS has not been good at involving people as patients or in decisions at a local or a national level, and this is an area where there are gains to be made in both health and politics.

We need to move to active care – active in the sense that as patients we feel more confident to look after ourselves and share decisions with clinicians. Decision-makers should embrace a proactive approach to public accountability, co-production and community development. Active communities must guide the development of local services. Clinicians should actively respond to needs and offer proactive care to people with long term conditions. We should be using well established mechanisms to predict whose health is most at risk and reach out to them, not wait for them to become ill.

Organisations which provide our care need to be active too; working in collaboration across organisational boundaries (not in competition) to share best practice; working with patients and commissioners to develop the services required. The best should help those trying to raise standards, not wait for them to fail. Active regulation should ensure problems are identified early, support is provided where needed but firm action is taken if that is not enough. We need regulation which does more than set up enquiries after the damage has been done.

Integration of Care

The boundaries between health and social care make little sense to anyone who needs both. Many are shocked to find that when they need social care they are subject to means testing. We need a national care service as much as we need a national health service. In time personal social care should be free at the point of need, as with health and for the same reasons, but the taxpayers are not yet ready to take this step in one go.

There is a wall between health and social care with different cultures, managed in radically different ways, and totally different accountability structures – not to mention health being national and free whilst social care is local and means tested. The failures of integration seen in bed blocking and unnecessary admissions cost money which could be better spent on improving care.

There should be an integrated assessment of need which is recognised across the country; recognising the needs of carers in the process; an assessment which is portable. The criteria used for the financial part of the assessment should be the same as for benefits entitlement and should be simple logical and consistent – including a single method for treatment of capital.

It remains the job of local government to decide how social care needs are to be met, reflecting local circumstances. There need to be incentives to ensure that measures which reduce the need for services – which often require a long term investment – are encouraged. This is not just about social services. It is also about housing, planning, education, transport and other policies under the control of national and local government.

Top down integration can be driven by making local authorities responsible for the overall wellbeing strategy for the area which will include health care requirements. Some services such as those for children or people with learning disabilities could be commissioned by them. Bottom up integration can be fostered by joint appointments, joint staff training and development, shared budgets, shared services and collocation. These have all been possible and have been used by the best but much stronger leadership is necessary and this has to come from elected representatives not from health bureaucrats!

Shared Responsibility and Co-production

We must all be encouraged, educated and supported to take more shared responsibility for our own wellbeing and the professionals must be better trained in how to bring this about. The many barriers which face those most likely to suffer poor health need to be addressed in ways which encourage involvement and improve access for disadvantaged groups. The principles of co-production, where care professionals and patients work together, must feature more in medical training and professional development. The model of care which leaves the patient a passive object of the clinician's attention is expensive and ineffective. Clinicians, especially Royal Colleges, must ensure that the idea of co-production is central to medical education.

Changing the Emphasis

Whilst we need more emphasis on prevention and less on cure we also have to shift where care is delivered. NHS culture is dominated by large hospitals and their large costs. Other systems work well with more care being delivered outside institutions, in more local settings and in the home, and medical and technological advances make this easier. If the appropriate infrastructure was in place outside hospitals then we could envisage perhaps a third of them closing and releasing resources back to fund local care.

Closing hospitals or even bits of hospitals raises local anxieties but the clinical model for concentration of high quality care in fewer centres of excellence combined with the ability to deliver a lot more care in more local settings has to be acknowledged and worked through. Effective engagement with clinical and community leadership is vital. Major investment in primary care is essential as is investment in public health, and that may imply less investment in PFI hospitals! Raising the capital to invest in building up community facilities remains a major issue. New sources of funding might be necessary such as allowing the issue of local "Health Bonds".

Choice and Information

Evidence shows that greater involvement of patients in their care improves outcomes. More patients want choice about how they are treated than about which organisation they are treated by. But choice and involvement must be, and can only be, built on better access to simple, officially sanctioned, information about care and treatment options and care pathways; entitlement and rights. This kind of information is not available for either health or social care and nobody has responsibility for its provisions – this should be local authorities.

It also requires us to have access to our own records, both health and other care. For the less able, such as the frail elderly or children, support and agency must be offered to assist with provision of information and so to enhance choice and involvement. The NHS has been slow to embrace the Internet. Portable electronic patient records, with access controlled by the patients, will not only drive process efficiencies but offer other avenues to personalise care and make it independent of organisational boundaries.

Communities need a greater say in local services, especially when changes to local services or closures are planned. This should be based on engagement rather than one-off artificial consultations – but the trade-off is that harder decisions can be made in the wider interest. An alliance between clinical leadership and local involvement is essential for extensive reconfiguration of services, such as closing an A&E or a birthing centre.

Commissioning and Rationing

Commissioning is the process where decisions are made about

how public money is spent and on what priorities are set and what standards apply. It is also about how we get best value for our public spending. Across local and central government commissioning has been separated from providing so decisions are not unduly influenced (though they must be informed) by provider power or conflicts of interest. This is hard in health care as the only place much of the necessary knowledge and expertise can be found is within the providers, so a more collaborative style to plan and then procure services is needed.

In such a model the local authority does the needs analysis and sets out the overall wellbeing strategy, guided by advice from public health experts. Care professionals specify requirements and establish care pathways. Those with expertise in procurement and contracting identify the providers, and develop the market to ensure the services are secured and best value is achieved. These functions interact but some are best done at national level, some at regional level and some locally. For some service designs, many clinicians may be involved (though not on a full time basis), for others a simple national template could be enough. It depends, and this flexibility mirrors other functions local authorities deal with, but not how the NHS operates. Over time, leadership and overall responsibility for commissioning has to move to local authorities, although they will no doubt delegate much of it.

Private or Public?

In both health and care services we have, and always have had, mixed economies with private as well as public providers of services, and we have seen scandalous failures in both sectors. In social care most is now privately provided. In health care there have been many recent attempts to increase the role for private sector providers and even for them to support commissioning.

Private providers can produce innovative and sometimes disruptive solutions which public providers do not often develop.

There are additional risks in employing commercial providers because of the external pressures to which they may be subject, and anyone procuring services needs to consider how these risks and benefits could be managed. Continuing with an established public provider will often be the least risk and that must be honestly reflected in decisions; best value meets preferred provider.

Similarly there is some (limited as yet) evidence that competition for services can improve quality, and for teeth and eyes we have had competition between providers for many years. It is not that competition has no part to play; it is that competition is not the best driving force for change in all services as the market evangelists try to argue. We do not need a proper 'market' system, even if we do need some elements of market behavior for some services.

Use What Works

If we have openness and transparency and publicly accountable decision-makers then they can be left to make decisions, as occurs with most public services – but not the NHS. There will be national quality standards which must be met and are regulated. But they should not need prescriptive guidance, sets of rules and regulations and imposition from performance management or an intrusive regulator. We need a quality regulator but not an economic regulator as well! We don't do that for education or social care so why do we do it for health?

Within this framework then, using what works, locally if relevant, does make sense. Patient-centred care requires a major shift in resources from acute to primary care and a seamless joining up of social and health care into a single integrated system, but by evolving what works not by one-off reorganisation – change coming from below where professionals learn to work together, more than from the top down, by evolving not revolving.

The Rt Hon Lord Hunt of Kings Heath, OBE

Our NHS: The Labour Party Challenge

Lord Hunt has held various positions in government, and was the Chief Executive of the NHS Confederation, Director of the National Association of Health Authorities and Trusts, and is currently the President of the Royal Society for Public Health, Chair of the Heart of England NHS Foundation Trust and Shadow Deputy Leader of the House of Lords.

Of all the U-turns made by the Government, the clearest is on the NHS. Yet despite a slower handover of commissioning to GP consortia – now to be renamed Clinical Commissioning Groups and the toning down of the competition remit of the economic regulator, Monitor, many threats remain. Labour will continue to expose the risks but the greater job will be to present a coherent vision of what it plans for the NHS.

It faced a similar challenge in 1997 and came through brilliantly. In 13 years, a crumbling edifice had been transformed into a real success story, with waiting times slashed and new services developed. How ironic, then, that the current Government feels free to make such sweeping and damaging changes to a remarkably healthy inheritance.

How is it that the current Conservative-led Government wants to cause so much turbulence? And how did Labour come to throw away what should have been its sharpest card at the election?

The Labour Party has always made the NHS its own. Its post-war creator, Aneurin Bevan promised that it would relieve suffering, and lift the shadow of fear of the financial consequences of illness from millions of people. Despite fierce opposition – not least from the BMA and the Tory party – the NHS did just that and enjoyed huge public support.

But nearly 50 years on, at the fag end of the Thatcher and Major years, it was deep in trouble with a chronic lack of resources, and long waiting times. The much vaunted Patients Charter had promised a maximum of 18 months but even such modest ambitions had not been delivered. There was a real sense of drift and decline with its future openly questioned.

Since Labour entered office in 1997, a remarkable transformation has occurred. 18 weeks is now the maximum waiting time and a huge investment has taken place in staff and new hospitals. Innovative services have been introduced like NHS Direct and Choose and Book, giving patients much more flexibility over hospital appointments. Not the least of our achievements has been the emphasis on clinical outcomes and patient safety.

These successes have been confirmed recently by the respected Commonwealth Fund of the US[32] which reported that the UK was the only one of 11 leading countries where wealth does not determine access to care. Even more remarkably, the fund reported that 92 % of respondents in the UK thought that if they became seriously ill, they were confident they would get the most effective treatment including drugs and diagnostic tests. This was the highest rating of all 11 countries.

The most recent British Social Attitudes[33] survey showed that satisfaction with the NHS is at the highest level ever. When Labour entered office in 1997, only a third of people (34%) were satisfied with the NHS. Yet by 2009, satisfaction stood at 64%, the highest level since the survey began.

Of course, that does not make the NHS perfect. There isn't such a system anywhere in the world. And we should be honest about some of our failings. Health inequalities remained stubbornly large. Poor outcomes in some cancers and stroke care have persisted although they are improving. The most recent report from the Ombudsman[34] has pointed up some serious concerns about the care of older people by the NHS.

But none of this is unsolvable. There was every reason to believe that patient outcomes would continue to improve. There were signs of Primary Care Trusts (PCTs) becoming more effective in commissioning services. With sensitive leadership, the NHS could have built on its impressive progress. Instead, the NHS is threatened with root and branch reforms which could so easily undo the real gains of recent years.

Government Proposals

The key feature is the abolition of PCTs and the creation of Clinical Commissioning Groups to commission £80 Bn worth of health care from providers. Hospitals will operate in a competitive market under the mantra "any willing provider". Anti-competitive practices will be policed by an economic regulator like OFGEM or OFCOM.

Mr Lansley believes that since GPs are responsible for generating most of the resources of the NHS, through their prescribing and referral to hospitals, it makes sense to put them in charge of the money as well. But it's doubtful if most GPs really want to or feel they have the skills to take on the responsibility of commissioning. It's even more unlikely that they will police fellow doctors who are unable to control demands on services. And patients are unlikely to take kindly to their GP's direct involvement in rationing services.

Little wonder that the Chairman of the Royal College of GPs,

Dr Clare Gerada, has said: "...making GPs the new rationers of NHS care could ruin the long-established bonds of trust between them and their patients..."

Of immediate concern, is whether the NHS can withstand the disruption caused by the setting up of a completely new system, whilst funding pressures are rising? The NHS may have a ring-fenced budget, but it has to make £20 Bn of efficiency savings in the next few years. On top of that, the severe cuts in adult social care budgets are playing havoc with the discharge of patients from hospitals.

There has been much critical comment on the lack of public accountability and indeed ability of GPs consortia to be effective commissioners. A return to post-code prescribing is also feared if NICE guidance ceases to be mandatory and Clinical Commissioning Groups come to differing views on whether to commission expensive new drugs or treatments. The removal of the private patient cap and the enforcement of competitive rules suggest that the private sector is going to play a major part in providing NHS services in the future. There are real concerns that the cherry picking of services will put the viability of many NHS trusts at risk.

Where We Went Wrong

Given the current high standing of the NHS, it is remarkable that the government feels able to take such a massive gamble. One possible factor is that despite Andy Burnham's valiant efforts, the Labour Government failed to get the NHS up as a top election issue. Neither the Conservative nor Liberal Democrats gave even a hint of the massive reform that was to come.

It has also to be admitted that a lot of momentum had gone out of our reforms by the time of the 2010 election. Most of the big thinking had taken place in our first term. I can vividly recall the wow factor when the NHS Plan[35] was published in 2000. This pivotal policy document was the product of an exciting partnership between key people in the NHS and Ministers and resulted in fundamental improvements.

Ten years on and we had lost ground as the experience of NHS Foundation Trusts shows. Their creation was a brave attempt to free the NHS from the debilitating control by hundreds of Whitehall targets. Of course, some targets – such as waiting times – are a fact of life in all public services and some are essential. But we overdid it. The beauty of foundation trusts in their accountability to local communities through a large membership was the potential to innovate and grow strong local links.

But the steam went out of the Foundation Trust programme which, at best, limped along. People were unsure whether ministers really meant business and the NHS was unenthusiastic about giving members a real stake in their local hospital.

This lack of progress was matched by the cultural reluctance of the NHS to give patients more control over their own treatment. Nowhere is the paternalistic attitude more visible than in the reluctance of many GPs to have opening hours that suit working people.

If we had managed to ground the NHS more firmly in its local roots; involve patients and energise PCTs, it is at least arguable that that ministers would be more wary of contemplating such a risky revolution. No wonder though, that the Coalition Government's proposals are deceptively clothed in warm words about patient choice. If the public had any notion that its result would be a post-code lottery, privatisation and long-waiting lists, then an outcry would surely follow.

Government Row-Back

First it is clear that the Government has been shaken by the opposition to proposed changes in the NHS. John Healey and his shadow health team deserve a lot of praise for exposing this. The slowdown of the programme and the recognition of the important input that hospital doctors can make is welcome. And the role of Monitor to promote integration of services as a counter-balance to the promotion of competition is a significant row-back. But fears remain, that the direction of travel is nonetheless towards a disjointed system where money is tight. Clinical Commissioning Groups are unwilling to take strategic decisions and the private sector hovering to pick up the juicy bits and let the rest go hang. For Labour, we have powerful and immediate opportunities for vigorous opposition to the Government's proposals. The Bill is currently before Parliament and there are good prospects in the House of Lords for defeating parts of the Bill.

Our first priority should be to undo or at least mitigate the market provisions contained in the Bill. Our aim should be to protect care pathways and the integration of services. Economic regulators should not be the driving force behind the NHS.

We should also be seeking to make Clinical Commissioning Groups properly accountable through the appointment of non-executives and others to the consortia boards. These groups should meet the good governance standards expected of any organisation that has responsibility for spending huge sums of our money.

Labour's credibility with NHS stakeholders will be enhanced if our opposition is backed up with a rigorous analysis of the damage that will be caused by the Government's proposals. We have to spell out the consequences of a market and of the potential variation in services. We need to be forensic in cataloguing the inevitable decline in provision. When waiting times start to slip – which is inevitable – we must be alert to perverse incentives encouraging NHS patients to go private.

Labour's Vision

In rejecting the worst excesses of a full blooded market, we have to show that our approach will work well for patients. We have to map out a vision of the future of an NHS which stands comparison with the best of consumer services in this country. Choice based on easily understandable information; services integrated across all its different parts; the patient's journey smooth and unimpeded.

Our last manifesto promised a series of guarantees to the public on waiting and access. This should be the foundation for our future health policy. We should develop our pioneering work on health outcomes to ensure information is avoidable and understandable for all specialities. Patient safety should be our number one priority. We need a much stronger approach to preventative healthcare and health inequalities. Much fun has been made about the Government's *nudge not nannying* approach to encourage us all to be more healthy. But we have to come up with a hard driven programme, which builds on the one good thing in the Government's proposals; the stronger involvement of local government.

We can't ignore the issue of care for older people. The recent Ombudsman's report is a real wake up call. We need to work very hard on the ideas we floated at the election about a national care service and transforming the way care is provided to elderly and disabled people.

Above all, we need to be on the side of the patient. Opening hours is a good case in point. GPs need to respond to the working patterns of their patients. NHS hospitals have to become a real 7 day a week operation. Above all, professionals have to build services round the patients.

Women, Equality and Poverty

Ellie Cumbo

All in This Together?
The Future of Gender Equality in
the Labour Party

Ellie works in criminal justice policy for a national charity, and has several years' experience campaigning to eliminate violence against women. She is committed to grassroots activism, having helped set up UK Feminista and served as a trustee of OBJECT. She sits on the General Committee for Hackney North and Stoke Newington CLP, and is also a qualified barrister, former student politician and member of a South London choir.

"Gender inequality is not a fight for women alone; it is a struggle that everyone has to engage with.....I believe it is the job of the party leader to develop policies that accept these as mainstream issues and ensure they are dealt with as such". This definitive expression of the mainstreaming approach to gender equality was given by Ed Miliband during the 2010 race for the Labour leadership, in response to the questions all five candidates were asked by grassroots activist group Lead4Women.

Like most of the other contenders, however, he also declared his support for 50% representation of women in the Shadow Cabinet, a Cabinet-level Shadow Women's Minister and particularly all-women shortlists. Acknowledging this apparent contradiction, he went on explicitly to characterise all-women shortlists as having a limited lifespan: "whilst we strive for the day when all-women shortlists are no longer needed because women's voices are heard just as clearly as men's, I will remain a strong supporter of all-women shortlists as a practical tool to help us embody our values and tackle inequality". This answers the questions he was asked, but also throws out new ones – about if and when that day might come, how we will know, and what happens afterwards.

This is a different dilemma from that which usually arises about positive discrimination, which is whether or not it is simply reverse sexism. That debate goes to the heart of different political philosophies and so will probably never reach consensus; liberal individualists (in all parties) struggle to see beyond the fact that the same opportunities are nominally available to all, meaning that outcomes are simply a matter of individual choices and trying to override them is perverse. By contrast, the Labour Party was built on an understanding that structural power imbalances blow this rather pat theory apart, and that the goal of representation is to speak for everyone.

So what remains unresolved is not the method, but the evaluation. At some point, a decision is going to have to be made about the shelf-life of all-women shortlists, and other gender equality strategies such as quotas for appointing party bodies and conference delegates. To at least begin this conversation now would be the mark of a fearless and far-sighted leader, who has a coherent theory on what fairness means in this context and doesn't avoid difficult subjects.

Of course, Labour should aspire to serious and automatic engagement throughout our party with issues that primarily or disproportionately affect women. Backbenchers should be as likely to campaign on sexual harassment on their constituency streets as traffic congestion. Critical obstacles to women's equality should be in every Labour thinker's sights, such as the widespread acceptance of gendered violence as an occupational hazard of being female, or an economy in which the hours, pay structures and wider culture all suggest men are still the default workers.

Whether or not these ambitious goals are eventually realised, is the end of gender-specific policy and representation really foreseeable? Or will there always be challenges faced by women that men might miss, however much they care about and communicate with women? And vice versa?

In the short time since they entered government, the Coalition have enacted a cautionary tale about the precipitate mainstreaming of gender-specific concerns. In his five years as Leader of the Opposition, David Cameron appeared to belong to a previously-unidentified species of pro-woman Tory. A stand-out example was his 2007 promise to take action against the social attitudes instrumental in Britain's high levels of rape. Many will have felt he missed the point somewhat in referring to this as "moral collapse" instead of "the same old misogyny", as if the intense public moralism of earlier periods had brought greater respect and dignity for women instead of the opposite. Even so, the radical impressiveness of proposed solutions such as including the notion of consent to sex in the sex education syllabus, from this of all sources, must be acknowledged.

Yet with the combined pressures of the financial crisis and the election that nobody won, a very different picture of Cameron and his team emerged. Despite the chants of "we're all in this together", it quickly emerged from research carried out by the then Shadow Minister for Women and Equalities, Yvette Cooper, that the planned cuts programme would cost women twice as much as men. As became evident when the Fawcett Society attempted a judicial review, on the basis that the government hadn't carried out the equality impact assessment required by law, it apparently had not occurred to them to check whether women were disproportionately affected. Meanwhile, anonymity for rape defendants, having sat almost unnoticed in the Liberal Democrat policy portfolio since 2006, had also made it into the coalition agreement without setting off any equality-conscious alarm bells. Lambasted by women's groups and Labour MPs for making it less likely that other victims and witnesses would come forward and for sending the message that rape allegations are inherently less reliable than any other kind, the policy was duly abandoned within just six months.

It nevertheless remains a memorable demonstration of what can go wrong when politicians mean well towards women but do not have a real understanding of gender at the heart of their internal culture and traditions. This may have signally failed to surprise anyone who didn't think either party had become feminist simply because the men who lead them play with their children and acknowledge the horror of rape. Though small pockets of sensible thinking on gender do exist in both parties, it is difficult to see how these can ever be absorbed into their core values when the direct participation of women has always been so poor. Not only do we currently have a Cabinet of just four women and a set of MPs in both governing parties that reflects this paucity, but the Conservatives in particular have a recent heritage of misogyny that is frankly eye-watering, such as John Redwood suggesting in 2007 that date rape isn't really a crime. How, in these circumstances, could the Government reasonably think they had this territory covered?

But perhaps the clearest and most compact example of failed mainstreaming is Boris Johnson's regime as the first Conservative Mayor of London. So confident were Johnson's team that modern, Metropolitan Conservatism could incorporate feminist concerns as a matter of course that one of their first actions on entering office was to axe the role of the Women's Adviser as a "1980s throwback". Two years later, his strategy on violence against women, 'The Way Forward', did indeed win plaudits for its ambitious scope and mastery of the global policy context. Yet bizarrely for feminist City Hall watchers, just one month later this same Mayor published a strategy to deal with health-specific inequalities which did not mention teenage pregnancy once. This was despite the fact that The Way Forward had detailed the research showing that a "sizeable minority of young people hold views condoning violence against women, particularly coercive sex", and a series of reports by the London Assembly's own Health and Public Services Committee explicitly linking high teenage pregnancy rates to sexist attitudes to sex.

Even more drastic was the disconnect revealed when the Mayor's public transport body, Transport for London, launched a safety campaign directed at women which featured a close-up image of a woman's tear-stained face as she is about to be raped, beside the words "Stop, no. Stop, please, no, please. Please stop taking unbooked minicabs". Voyeuristic and victim-blaming, the poster's rhetorical device of imitating the woman's plaintive cries even managed to suggest equivalence between making the wrong transport decision and the act of rape. Heavily criticised for its insensitivity to London's thousands of rape victims, it was also extraordinarily off-message from a Mayor who in The Way Forward had set out a commitment to "transform the cultures and traditions that tolerate and perpetuate violence against women".

Far from embedding gender-awareness throughout the London governance machine, then, it seems that the removal of a focal point of knowledge and leadership on these issues, in the form of the Women's Adviser, has led to inconsistency, missed opportunities and the entrenchment of harmful attitudes.

The problem with the mainstreaming approach to gender-specific policy is not that it is ideologically the wrong thing to do – quite the opposite – but that the evidence shows it cannot happen without self-awareness, intelligence and, crucially, the safeguard of direct representation. For this reason, we must be cautious about dispensing with our own gender equality strategies, or at least about doing so for good. All-women shortlists should surely not be thrown out, but kept in the cupboard for whenever our pool of candidates would otherwise be seriously imbalanced in favour of men. And, for the sake of consistency, the same should apply if the imbalance is in favour of women: a Parliament of 75% women discussing prostate cancer or domestic violence towards men would surely make uncomfortable viewing.

Of course it is a naïve solution to assume that membership of a gender is a qualification to speak for all the others. It is possible, though unlikely, that the party could field 300 female candidates at the next general election who have encountered minimal sexism in their entire lives and don't believe it exists. Equally, no fair-minded feminist should hesitate to acknowledge the role of equality-conscious men in some of the strides women have taken in recent decades, and not only in our party. But permanently entrenching gender parity into our party is the best solution we have, both to outright gender inequality, and to the risk that there will always be differences in how men and women experience the same policies. Dispensing with direct representation of women seems too likely to lead to inevitable breakdown; instead of being like removing the stabilisers from a bike, it would be akin to stealing one of the wheels.

In the meantime, the mission to make equality issues into mainstream concerns has to start in earnest and, crucially, must start with the abandonment of any complacency about our record. On women and the economy, despite the excellent work of Cooper and colleagues such as Rachel Reeves, it seems that confident insight into the unique challenges faced by women do not yet come naturally to all corners of the party. The emerging Blue Labour strain of thought has corralled key previously-marginalised voices into a narrative that has much to offer, particularly around the importance of community and the private sphere. It is, however, deeply regrettable that it has taken so long to clarify its support for feminism.

In *The Labour tradition and the politics of paradox*, edited by four men and with just three female contributors out of 20, Jonathan Rutherford implicates women's economic independence in an "inter-generational rupture" that has left men and women more stressed and isolated than previous generations. This isn't necessarily untrue, but it fails to acknowledge the ludicrously obvious benefits for abused women, widowed women, gay women, women who like being single and both men and women who want to conduct relationships with each other on terms of equality, none of whom have historically fared well when the state backs off. No Labour party deserving of the name should hesitate to celebrate, let alone defend women's liberation, and this should have been tightly woven into Blue Labour's narrative from the start.

We also have work to do if we are to reclaim the clear lead we once had on tackling gender-based violence. At Prime Minister's Questions in July 2011, Ed Miliband took a strong stand in favour of retaining the DNA database as a crucial weapon in the fight to increase the rape conviction rate. This was a cause he championed during the leadership campaign too; it is clearly a genuine personal priority. But he must next develop this position to incorporate all the cases of rape and sexual violence where the DNA database won't help, and something more complex and challenging is needed.

Feminists have fought hard to establish that the majority of rapes are committed by someone known to the victim; in such cases it is almost inevitably the consent of the complainant, and not the identity of the accused, that is in question. Evidence in such cases is difficult, but not impossible to gather: funding more Sexual Abuse and Rape Crisis Centres, with their forensic expertise, is crucial to increasing the conviction rate.

But there is another, inadequately scrutinised problem here:

when the Fawcett Society published local rape conviction rates in 2004, 2006 and 2007, it emerged that some police areas consistently see a much lower proportion (as opposed to number) of cases end in conviction than others. Why should Cambridgeshire regularly have a conviction rate that is around a quarter of that that in Cleveland, for example? There is more than one hypothesis available; it could be due to varying levels of progressiveness in police attitudes, or perhaps inconsistent use of the charging standard meaning that prosecutors in some areas either dismiss cases that might have been seen as viable elsewhere, or give victims false hope by taking hopeless cases to court. In any case, this was an under-valued piece of research whose time may be about to come with the introduction of locally-elected Policing and Crime Commissioners, and Labour should be the party to make good on its concern for crime victims by applying the pressure for change. Justice for victims of sexual crime is already too elusive; it shouldn't be a postcode lottery too.

Finally, at an even more fundamental level, we should draw on the expertise of the women's sector to explore the apparently revolutionary notion that gender-based violence is not inevitable. Organisations like the End Violence Against Women coalition have considerable knowledge to impart around the reasons why some people become abusers, the social factors that facilitate this and the mechanisms that might stop it, as in their recent call on Secretary of State for Education, Michael Gove, to make schools central in combating sexual violence between young people. This is the future of the global campaign to free women from the injustice of gender-based violence; since it would also free the economy from its consequences, however, it is likely to be of immense interest to the right if they should start paying attention before we do. Labour should make it an urgent priority to become the party of prevention.

Ideally, the future of Labour feminism is both a new confidence that our efforts to ensure gender equality in our structures have made a difference, and will continue to do so, and an acceptance that this work is not yet done. Recent political history is filled with warnings for any party that believes representing women adequately is simple, or happens by accident. In this context, strategies like all-women shortlists should be seen not as merely temporary, necessary evils but as innovations that no other party could produce, and of which Labour should be proud. Used judiciously, they can help Labour lock into the needs of our diverse society more effectively than any other party for a long time to come.

At the same time, we must see meaningful efforts towards the genuine mainstreaming of gender-awareness throughout the party, through brave and creative ideas that will actually improve the lives of ordinary people who also happen to be women. This cannot happen if we are complacent on gendered issues; given our own recent lapses and the obvious determination of the Coalition to take this ground from us, however incompetently, neither we nor the country's women can afford that.

Baroness Mary Goudie of Roundwood

Can We End Poverty Globally?
Asking the Hard Questions

Baroness Goudie is Chair of the Women Leaders' Council to Fight Human Trafficking at the United Nations. She launched the global initiative to fight human trafficking and is involved with the G8 and G20 promoting the role of women and children in the global economy. She is actively engaged in numerous philanthropic organisations including her role as a member of the Executive and Board of Directors of Vital Voices Global Partnership. In recognition of her work, she was awarded the 2010 GlobalPower Award by the Center for Women Policy Studies.

Before we begin to answer the question "can we end poverty globally?" we need to ask ourselves two other hard questions and be willing to answer them honestly. First, we need to ask ourselves if our global poverty reduction strategy to date has worked? Secondly, if we are willing to do things differently going forward?

Here are my answers. I think our overseas aid strategy hasn't worked as well as it could, and that we must take a different path in order to ensure that Britain continues to be a leader in crafting a global solution that helps families, communities and countries build sustainable, healthy and violence free futures.

Britain must be a world leader on these issues, and that leadership must span governments, whether that government is Labour, Conservative or Liberal. Playing this global role is in our national interest, as it helps ensure stability at home and around the world. But, having said that, Labour is uniquely situated to lead on these global meta-issues. We were the first party in Britain to grapple with these issues and we were the first to establish a separate government department to focus on addressing development needs, now known as the Department for International Development (DFID).

In order to build upon Labour's legacy in the arena of overseas aid, we must continue to be bold and innovative. Providing aid to those in need cannot be our goal; it is an important step towards our goal of transforming countries and communities to self-sufficiency and competitiveness.

We need fewer handouts and better results. While there are many success stories, and evidence of effective programs, there is much more to do to reach our goals. In this challenging financial and political environment, where we cannot afford to waste any resource, human or otherwise, we need overseas aid that helps countries solve their problems and build public and private infrastructure to solve problems, not create cultures of complacency and dependency.

We need to clarify our goals, both globally and on a country or sectoral basis, and then create measurements for the effectiveness of aid in meeting those goals. Putting it simply, we need to define what success will look like, and what kind of impact we want to have with our aid.

To do this, we need to work with other governments, donors, non-governmental organisations (NGOs), and the private sector to design smart, effective and bold solutions that will bring people out of poverty and improve a country's infrastructure and ability to compete globally. As stewards of British taxpayer's money, we must demand the most effective use of the funds targeted to address global issues.

Women are central to aid reform

Any strategy we pursue needs to involve women and girls. We must see women as effective agents of change, not just beneficiaries of our aid. Women, who comprise over 50 percent of the world's population, perform 60 percent of the world's work, but only earn 5 percent of the world's income. Rural women produce half of the world's food and in developing countries, between 60 and 80 percent of food crops. Globally, 1.4 billion people subsist on less than £1 per day. Most of them (829 million) are women. The majority of the unschooled are women and 75 percent of those who are illiterate are women. In short, in order to solve the problems that are at the heart of overseas aid, we must focus on women and girls, and involve them in developing solutions that work. Women – still one of the world's great untapped resources – are central to building global peace and prosperity. Despite the imbalance in income, women invest 90 percent of their income in their families and communities compared to men who invest only 30 to 40 percent. According to the World Economic Forum Gender Gap Report, the most prosperous countries are those where the gaps between men and women on a series of measures are narrowest. If our overseas aid is successful at valuing women and girls, we will have better outcomes across the board.

Investing in women and girls can make a big difference. When a girl in a developing world receives seven or more years of education, she will marry four years later and have 2.2 fewer children. An extra year of primary school boosts girls' eventual wages by 10 to 20 percent; an additional year of secondary school boosts her wages by 15 to 25 percent. Research has shown a consistent relationship in developing countries between better infant and child health and higher levels of schooling among mothers. Asian Pacific countries alone lose £26 billion to £30 billion annually in GDP because of the untapped potential of women in those economies.

Investing in results

There are hard questions ahead of us. We need to rethink where we invest our aid. We need to carefully consider how to make decisions regarding aid that will have the biggest impact on solving seemingly intractable problems. While there are needs everywhere in the world, we must think long and hard about where Britain can have the biggest impact and deliver results.

This may mean that we don't give the same amount of aid to countries that have received aid before, or that we structure our aid differently. We should reward countries that are making progress and meeting goals. But, looking at results and working backwards may be the best way to proceed. Structuring our aid to help reach our development goals and targets, and then working backwards, may be the most effective approach. Do we need to provide overseas assistance to countries with strong emerging economies like Brazil, China, Russia and India? Do we need to put conditions on any of our aid? Should we demand that all countries take all steps necessary to fight human trafficking and child marriage? We need to carefully evaluate these questions.

In addition, our investment must be transparent and we must measure results. We should consider annual, in-depth evaluators to look at aid, its effectiveness and whether what we are doing on a country by country basis helps us meet our collective goals of ending poverty.

Finding the right partners

We must, however, make sure we do this right. The funds we invest must be invested in the right programmatic work and get to the right people.

First, we must ensure that we co-ordinate across our various governmental departments, so that our development aid is co-ordinated with any other actions or aid our government is undertaking in a particular country or community.

Second, we need strong partners from every sector. It is important that we continue Britain's leadership in strong multilateral international organizations, such as the United Nations, the International Labour Organisation, the European Union, the Organization for Economic Co-operation and Development, as well as the World Bank and the International Monetary Fund, to name a few. As a leader in this global community, we must help shape a common set of goals, and place those goals within the context of what other countries and multinational entities are doing so that we can better co-ordinate our collective work.

Third, we need to engage the private sector, and be innovative in how public-private partnerships can leverage resources and help drive change. This may mean incentives for companies to work with governments on developing technologies that work.

Fourth, it is critical to find strong NGO partners on the ground, partners who are knowledgeable about needs and capacities, and can reach those who need our help. We need to partner with NGOs that are credible in this country, can work across multiple sectors and can deliver results and are transparent in their financial dealings. We must work with NGOs that meet these criteria, so that the funds we invest are used in the most effective manner. This means taking a hard look at all of our current partners and evaluating them, with a willingness to make decisions about who is most effective at ensuring that we meet our goals using government resources. If these NGOs do not meet our criteria, we need to find out why, and see if we are working with the right groups.

What should our programmatic goals be?

There are many ways to focus aid, but if we centre our approach on addressing issues faced by women and girls, there is some key programmatic work to be done here.

First, it is important that we address legal barriers that women face, whether those barriers are to property ownership, citizenships rights, access to capital or access to education. We must promote our values of fair treatment for all, and that means looking at how countries address issues such as labour standards, domestic violence, human trafficking and child marriage. We might want to look at how to amplify the United States government's annual Trafficking in Persons (TIP) report, which looks at practices in 184 countries, so that we understand what is occurring on the ground in countries receiving our aid.

Second, we should continue effective aid programs that support maternal and child health, family planning and nutrition, education and fighting diseases such as malaria, HIV/AIDS and tuberculosis. We must also work to improve existing health care systems and use innovative new technologies – like mobile phones – to deliver health information.

Third, we should begin to focus on issues that have arisen as a result of global climate change. Our development aid should be 'green' so that we are not contributing to the devastating effects of climate change, especially on the daily lives of women. In many countries, women already walk miles for water and firewood, and climate change will make this daily task even more difficult. Further, developing clean energy. growth and development can spur economic growth and strong partnerships with the private sector.

Fourth, we should look at investments in food security to strengthen the world's food supply. Women are critical to these efforts as women are the majority of small holder farmers in sub-Saharan Africa and worldwide have access to only 10 percent of all credit and 1 percent of credit in the agricultural sector. This could go hand in hand with efforts to reform land tenure and property rights, as well as providing farmers with the technical assistance and inputs they need to grow more food and get it to market.

Fifth, we should ensure that our programs spur economic growth and entrepreneurship, and ensure that women have financial identities. This includes microfinance for women farmers and entrepreneurs but also access to capital and skills development so that women can graduate to small and medium sized businesses over time.

Finally, we need to ensure that there are women represented in every body that makes these decisions – whether at the global, national, or community level. Having women at every table,

and in every hall, board room, and legislature, makes a difference in terms of the policy and programmatic issues that get raised. We cannot afford to make decisions without women being represented and part of the solution

We provide aid in many post-conflict countries and it is particularly important that there are women involved in the peace process. The views, concerns, and perspectives that women have are more often taken into account and addressed when there are women involved in the peace process and women's voices are heard. Women raise different issues in the peace process, including war related sexual violence; accountability and justice; creating more economic opportunities for women; reintegration of men into a changed family dynamic and social structure. These are issues that are critically important to rebuilding a society where aid can be effectively invested and countries can move forward.

This is the right time for Labour to lead on these issues and to take fresh approach that can serve all of us well for years to come.

The Green Agenda

William Bain MP

Justice and Growth: Labour's Agenda on Food Security

William was elected to Parliament in 2009 after being selected as the Labour candidate in the Glasgow North East by-election after the Speaker of the House of Commons, Michael Martin, resigned. William is a former Law lecturer. He served as PPS to Sadiq Khan in the Department for Transport, and as Shadow Transport Minister between May-Oct 2010. He is currently Shadow Minister for Environment, Food and Rural Affairs. His policy interests are the economy, welfare, the EU, US and China, and international development.

In its period in government, Labour achieved a great deal on the natural environment – joining with other governments to adopt binding climate change reduction targets at Kyoto, the development of a new agenda on renewable energy and clean coal technology, the first national food plan for fifty years, a ban on hunting with hounds, together with laws on animal welfare and protection of the marine environment.

Now, in opposition, preparing for a probable general election in 2015, we have the opportunity to meet and match new challenges in generating new jobs in environmental industries, tackling food insecurity, and reducing the impact of greenhouse gas emissions throughout food production chains and other spheres of economic activity.

Our starting point must be valuing the natural environment. The Tory-led Government is cutting £2bn from departmental expenditure on the natural environment over the period of the comprehensive spending review. The UN Environmental Programme has established that loss of ecosystem services through deforestation and other degradation, could result in up to a 25% loss in global food production by 2050, with a consequential surge in levels of hunger and poverty. Labour must demonstrate renewed leadership on this issue as we did over climate change in the last decade. The OECD in its report on the green economy, recommended a wider measure of economic progress beyond mere GDP, into areas such as clean air and water, and biodiversity. It concluded that developed countries should increase the issuance of green bonds beyond the combined current levels of $11bn per annum. Hundreds of billions of dollars of new investment could drive growth in new and environmentally sustainable industries.

Agriculture is one of the most significant parts of the UK economy. It directly employs over half a million people and contributes over £7 billion directly to the UK economy each year, with the agri-food sector constituting almost 6.7% of economic output. It is increasingly recognised that farmland has a wider function than simply agricultural production. In particular, it has a role in water protection and in sustaining landscapes and habitats that are rich in biodiversity.

As the Food 2030 and Foresight reports have made clear, world population growth of between 2 to 3 billion in the next four decades will necessitate an increase in global food production in the region of 70%, but that must be sustainable, with incentives for water recycling, more efficient use of soil, and energy efficiency measures in agricultural production. The World

Economic Forum in its 2011 report on Global Risks describes the water-food-energy nexus as one of the key drivers of future social and economic instability, which must be overcome by policy makers. The International Food Policy Research Institute expects a 30% increase in demand for water, and the International Energy Agency (IEA) forecasts that the world economy will require at least 40% more energy by 2030. It questions the sustainability of the production of crops for first generation bio-fuels – were current levels of demand to be maintained – involving between 20 to 100% of the total quantity of water currently used in global agriculture.

Agriculture accounts for 14% of global greenhouse emissions, and in 2006 the food supply chain was responsible for 160 million tonnes of carbon dioxide-equivalent emissions: one third came from primary production; a further third came from manufacturing, distribution and the sale of food; and a final third came from household food emissions and emissions embedded in imported food. Just as every other part of our economy is making its contribution to tackling climate change, by reducing emissions by 34% by 2020 and by 80% by 2050, so too must agriculture. Currently, under the low-carbon transition plan, agriculture in England has an emissions reduction target of 3 million tonnes by 2020.

Questions have arisen over the use of soya in animal feed as a source of protein and the growth of crops for the production of bio-fuels. In some parts of the world, such as Brazil, soya production has become connected with deforestation and environmental damage, amounting to almost 80% of Brazil's greenhouse gas emissions. Friends of the Earth pointed out in its recent analysis that global soya bean production increased by 4.6% annually from 1961 until 2007 and reached an average annual production of 217.6 million tonnes between 2005 and 2007. World production of soya beans is predicted to increase by 2.2% annually to 371.3 million tonnes by 2030.

The market for meat is increasing in other continents, but has declined in the UK since 2003. In 1985, the average Chinese consumer ate 20 kg of meat a year; now he or she eats more than 50 kg a year. In developing countries as a whole, the demand for meat has doubled since 1980. As the 2009 UN Food and Agriculture Organisation report on the State of Food and Agriculture finds, between 1980 and 2007, China increased its production of meat by more than sixfold. Today it accounts for nearly 50% of meat production in developing countries and 31% of world production. Brazil expanded meat production by a factor of almost four, and now contributes 11% of developing country meat production and 7% of global production.

But agriculture also has a central role in driving an increase in global economic growth, food security and poverty reduction. According to the 2009 FAO report, agricultural productivity growth has positive effects for the poor in three areas: lower prices for consumers; higher incomes for producers; and growth multiplier effects through the rest of the economy, as demand for other goods and services increases. It also establishes that agricultural growth reduces poverty more strongly than growth in other sectors.

Recent research by Julian Alston, published by the OECD, has found that the world has benefited greatly from productivity growth in agriculture, a substantial amount of which has been enabled by technological change resulting from public and private investments in agricultural research and development, although he encourages countries to increase their levels of investment in such R&D. The FAO has recently published research on the integration of food and energy production as an effective means of combining greater food security with poverty reduction for developing nations. Through supporting tax incentives, input subsidies, and technical support for smallholder farms to grow both food and sustainable energy crops, leading to more efficient water and soil use, and a reduction in greenhouse gas emissions. A 2009 Chatham House report by Alex Evans established that half a billion people across the world face chronic shortfalls of water, likely to rise above 4 billion people by 2050. As a result of climate change, but also from unsustainable extraction from rivers, lakes and groundwater, leaving food production particularly exposed, and called for a system shift away from an inputs-focused approach to agriculture, to a knowledge-based approach instead, together with a recognition of the importance of food security in any revised WTO rules emerging from the Doha round.

Currently, about 9% of total UK and EU greenhouse gas emissions stem from agriculture. That represents a 2% reduction from comparable statistics from 1990. The Commission's 2009 White Paper indicates that agricultural emissions in the 27 EU member states reduced by 20% between 1990 and 2007 owing to the marked decline in livestock numbers, more efficient application of fertilisers and better manure management. This 20% fall in emissions from agriculture is significantly higher than the 11% reduction in emissions in all EU sectors, and contrasts with the 17% increase in global emissions stemming from agriculture.

The cross-compliance and rural development measures of the EU's common agricultural policy are assisting in the further reduction of agricultural climate change emissions, through the modernising farms programme, extending the use of energy-efficient equipment and buildings, expanding the available support to generate biogas through anaerobic digestion, and the compensatory measures for farmers who assist in environmental protection through agri-environment schemes under Pillar 2 of the Common Agricultural Policy.

Labour should champion measures to assist the food industry make further reductions in their greenhouse gas emissions. The technology is there to achieve this, but leadership coupled with action by government is essential. As the Committee on Climate

Change made clear in their Fourth Carbon Budget and their progress report on the Third Carbon Budget, agriculture in Britain is achieving annualised emission reductions of 1% per year, in line with the Low Carbon Transition Plan introduced by Labour, but nowhere near the potential further abatement required to meet the UK's overall emission reduction targets by 2030. Labour can outflank the Government on a sustainable food policy by supporting policies for increased incentives to drive the take up of renewable energy on farms, innovative land, soil, and water use, anaerobic digestion, and initiatives to change consumer behaviour such as greater production and consumption of fruit and vegetables as in WWF's Livewell Report, and slashing levels of food waste, currently costed at £5bn per year.

The FAO's agriculture and commodity prices report from 2009 found that in June 2008, the prices of basic foods on international markets reached their highest levels for 30 years, threatening the food security of the poor worldwide. In 2007 and 2008, mainly because of high food prices, an additional 115 million people were pushed into chronic hunger. Volatility in food supply and pricing impedes meeting the challenges of feeding a predicted global population of 9 billion people by 2050, with a particular emphasis on population growth in Africa. The UN Food and Agriculture Organisation outlined in its June 2011 report on Crop Prospects that levels of food insecurity have reached alarming levels in East Africa, and remains a concern in Western Africa. In Africa as a whole, some 23 countries are in need of external assistance to feed their populations, owing to extreme swings in weather, population displacement or internal strife. As US Secretary of State, Hillary Clinton, told the FAO in Rome on 6 May, some 44 million people across the globe were pushed into poverty as a result of price volatility from June 2010. The OECD Secretary-General, Angel Gurria, spoke in early June at the Forum of the Americas, of the imperative of increasing public and private sector agricultural investment and an end to export bans.

There is a debate currently raging among NGOs and economists about the contribution of commodity price speculation and trading in commodity derivatives to the volatility in global food prices since 2006, and the predicted rise of 30% in global food prices over the next decade estimated by the OECD and the UN Food and Agriculture Organisation. There is evidence that the degree of speculation on food derivatives contracts by index funds increased between 2003 and 2007, and appreciably so in the first half of 2008, when global prices spiked by 25%.

Oxfam and the World Development Movement are engaged in a campaign to regulate commodity speculation, along the principles set out in the Dodd-Frank legislation signed by President Obama in the US last March, of greater transparency in the trade in over-the-counter derivates, amounting to between 80-90% of US commodity derivative sales, worth in total $9trillion per annum. Done without the involvement of the financial markets; and of regulation in terms of the value of the positions which individual investors or financial institutions may hold. Although the Bank for International Settlements estimated in 2010 that commodity speculation only accounted for 0.5% of the global derivatives trading market, financial institutions account for 96% of the trade in commodity derivatives – Goldman Sachs, Morgan Stanley, Barclays Capital, JP Morgan and Deutsche Bank. Congress and the US Administration are in discussions about how to implement the Dodd-Frank commitments, with the Commodity Futures Trading Commission consulting on new rules to reform regulation of derivative markets, including a limitation on proprietary trading and the size of positions within commodity markets which funds and financial institutions may hold.

Nevertheless, other economists of global stature, such as Paul Krugman, have downplayed the role of speculation on the spike in food prices in 2006-8, preferring instead to consider the effects of global warming on changing weather patterns, and any enduring impact now.

Key to Labour's response is to acknowledge that the relationship between oil prices and food prices is an increasingly close one. An oil price hike sparks movements in index funds, and produces a consequential rise in agricultural commodity prices. There may be a dispute over whether this drives or is in spite of the effects of a more erratic global climate on crop yields and harvests, but the case for urging the G20 to take further action to render transparent over the counter derivative trading is one Labour should support.

Labour should also champion freer and fairer trade as a means of lowering domestic food prices, and securing economic justice for the developing world. This would be best aided by a successful completion of the WTO Doha Round on trade liberalisation for the developing world, with the EU displaying stronger leadership on ending unjustifiable subsidies. Agriculture spending accounts for 41% of the EU's current financial perspective, or €55 billion a year. With pressures to lower the EU budget, agriculture cannot be immune from efficiencies, and a renewed focus on supporting innovation and research to promote greater food security will be required, in line with the communiqué from G20 Agriculture Ministers at their recent summit in Paris. But unlike DEFRA in the UK, which will be reducing the overall departmental evidence budget, which incorporates research and development, by 20% by 2014-15, other EU agriculture must display far greater foresight in investing in food science and innovation.

Currently, the EU pays 100,000 cotton farmers $2.51 per pound of cotton produced, yet the global price of cotton has dipped as low as $1.50 per pound in the past twelve months. It has been established that the overall total of cotton production subsidies from the United States and the EU has approached $32 billion in the past nine years, which Fairtrade estimates has cost

West African farmers $250 million in annual lost income over that period. We should strongly support reform of the EU Common Agricultural Policy to remove such trade distorting subsidies.

Conclusion

Many of Labour's natural supporters in the green and environmental movement became disillusioned in our final years in office, and many voters concerned about the natural environment drifted away at the last General Election. To win back their trust and support, Labour must develop the themes and produce detailed policy ideas to show how green growth is the best growth that Government can facilitate, and be bold in how the power of markets and capital can be harnessed and shaped by national and international co-operation to increase it. In food policy, we must make global markets fairer and more resilient and transparent, we must show long-term leadership in the form of a sustainable diet which promotes better public health and environmental outcomes, and provide consequential subsidies in innovation and research that solve the conjoined challenges of increasing food production, cutting greenhouse gas emissions, and taking care of the scare resources of water and energy. If we do so, we can be confident of securing justice for this generation, and for those that follow.

Kieran Roberts

Sustainable Socialism

*Kieran is an environmental campaigner, former Labour PCC,
Vice Chair of North West Young Labour and is reading LLB
Law with Politics at the University of Manchester.*

When I was given the opportunity to contribute to this book,
I instinctively wanted to write about how Labour would do
best to help avert environmental catastrophe and to say I'm late
to the party would be a gross understatement. Literally
thousands write and speak about this topic and much of it gets
lost in the noise. The green movement has swelled since its days
in the wilderness but for voters, the environment is not the
political priority that most campaigners argue it should be, and
far from it. So why is the green message failing to resonate and
ultimately be implemented? Fortunately, most people believe in
climate change and don't want to see the natural world depleted.
At fault then is the communication of the solutions and the lack
of political leadership. In this chapter, I want to set out how
Labour can overcome both and set out a progressive, electable
vision on the environment.

There are two fatally inaccurate perceptions of environmentalism:

that it's either a bourgeois or hippy concern and that sustainable development is regressive – economically and materialistically. Busting these myths and pursuing a radical environmental agenda should be natural Labour territory but it's been something we've never managed to completely understand. In government, we set green targets for businesses but didn't sufficiently regulate them, we designated marine conservation zones but stood idly by as our fish stocks were exhausted and the poor communication of our policies resulted in an unconvinced and unsupportive electorate. That result was not entirely fair. It took a Labour Government to sign the Climate Change Act in to law; the most progressive environmental legislation in modern British history. Whilst there are areas of our record to defend, we must recognise where we fell short and also understand why we had the appearance of a party that didn't practice what it preached. Whilst aiming for ambitious carbon reductions, we allowed new coal stations and pushed for more airport expansions, and by conveying our message largely in terms of carbon, it was an abstract message that was near impossible to relate to. Who is it that suffers from fuel poverty? Who is it that disproportionately suffers from water pollution? Who is it that already suffers from the effects of climate change? And who is it that contributes the least? Labour must understand and communicate the fact that in protecting our environment, we protect the poorest and most vulnerable in our societies. Environmentalism is a prerequisite for social justice. The task is immense but so are the opportunities. There are a number of realistic yet radical steps which we can take in the following areas – the economy, energy, and ecology – that will begin meeting the challenge for the first time in British history.

Economy
GDP is viewed by many as a grossly distorted picture and we ignore its failings at our peril. GDP was first developed by Simon

Kuznets for a US Congress report in 1934. At the time, he warned not to use it as a measure for welfare but it has become something far more dangerous than that. It is seen by too many now as a measure of worth. Are rainforests, the world's air-conditioning system, only worth something when they're converted in to toilet roll? The problem in measuring economic transactions indiscriminately is that it fails to take in to account the real worth of something. In the pursuit of increasing GDP for economic growth, governments, like GDP, have failed to take in to account that worth as well. We must begin to add nature's services to our balance sheets and impressively, DEFRA have begun to embark on this. This approach however needs to be taken in every government department and not stop short at DEFRA, so as Ed Miliband said, the Treasury can become an Office for the Environment, factoring in the environmental impact of every spending decision it makes. My favourite quote of any politician sums up the limit of GDP more thoroughly than I ever could. Robert Kennedy said this: "GDP does not allow for the health of our children, the quality of their education, or the joy of their play. It measures neither our wit nor our courage; neither our wisdom nor our learning; neither our compassion nor our devotion to our country. It measures everything, in short, except that which makes life worthwhile". Our environment: the food we eat, the air we breathe and the land we live in is all central to this. Instead of relentlessly pursuing increasing GDP, Labour must have the courage to recognise and overcome its limitations and instead pursue "that which makes life worthwhile".

GDP is a product of the free-market society which is another sacred cow most environmentalists would be happy to slay. The principal reason for this is because the market has been such a powerful force for environmental destruction. What Labour must embrace is that the market is also, apart from nature, the most powerful force for change. Businesses are beginning to become greener, not necessarily due to any environmental concern but because of increasing consumer demand. So right now is a perfect opportunity for Labour to utilise the market to green ends yet remain business friendly. The approach should be threefold.

For businesses, the environment is as much a financial concern as it is an ethical one. Labour must create a framework which provides immediate help to businesses that want to save money through increasing efficiency and reducing waste. That means rewarding sustainability, providing grants for energy efficiency and turning waste in to a financial liability. Businesses are already doing this. Take DuPont for example. Over 10 years, they have reduced emissions by 60 per cent and as a result, increased productivity by 30 per cent and saved £1.2 billion in efficiencies. All businesses should be embarking on this and Labour can be the champion of them. One step to doing this would be leading by example. Why aren't hospitals, schools, Sure Start centres and Labour offices powered by renewable energy? If Labour take the DuPont approach to the services it runs, it will save money through efficiency and shatter the image that Labour doesn't practice what it preaches.

As well as giving power to businesses to become greener, we must give power to the consumer. A perverse situation exists at the moment in which it is easier for the richer to be green than the poorer. This is where environmentalism and social justice become indistinguishable and this is territory for Labour to seize. As I highlighted the opportunity to help businesses reduce waste, the same applies to the consumer. Consumers don't want to waste. Excessive packaging is forced on them and simply recycling it, although more sustainable, is not ideal. If consumers had the option to take their empty packaging back to the shops it came from, those businesses would have no choice but to dispose of it. It would then be in their interest to start reducing the excesses and waste. A second simple step to reducing so-called consumer waste would be to introduce a plastic bag tax. Perhaps for fear of a backlash, Labour didn't introduce one whilst in power but we need only look to Ireland to see why they needed to. In 2002 when they introduced their plastic bag tax, within weeks plastic bag use declined by 94 per cent. That statistic speaks for itself.

Despite the huge success of Ireland's plastic bag tax, 'green taxes' are criticised for being ineffective and are tarred with the same brush as stealth taxes. Surprisingly, green taxes actually fell between 1997 and 2009 from 9.5 to 7.9 percent of total receipts, but that alone is not enough to shed this misconception. What would achieve this, is a guarantee that all revenues from green taxes will be spent pursuing green policies. Regardless of this, taxation still remains the best method for reducing pollution and increasing sustainability. If businesses face painful financial losses for polluting, they will respond and reduce it. If greater efficiency and reduced waste is the carrot, taxing pollution is the stick. That is why the market is such a powerful force for change and that's why Labour should not be afraid to embrace it.

Energy
If we want to deal with climate change, our energy policy should be our priority. Even if you don't believe that man-made climate change is happening, we need to end our dependency on fossil fuels due to the simple fact that before long, they will run out. Before we consider alternative energy production, we need to focus on ending the waste of what we already produce.

Before we even begin to consume the energy we require, one third of it has already been wasted. Due to the distance it has to travel from the centralised power stations to our homes and offices, this staggering proportion is lost through power lines and waste heat from cooling towers. This accounts for a fifth of the UK's carbon dioxide emissions alone. Fortunately, the work of Tory and Liberal Democrat councillors in Woking shows us the way around this problem. Woking has pioneered micro-generation. They've built over 60 small-scale power generators, ended their reliance on the grid, have cut their energy use by half and reduced their carbon emissions by 77 per cent since 1990. The savings made from these measures were recycled each year and re-invested into further energy saving measures. In doing this, the system is no more expensive than the previous one. The initial barrier to this was that the council had to lay private wires to all the buildings that took its electricity due to regulations protecting the larger power stations. Scrapping that regulation can open up the chance for more towns to follow Woking's example, reducing energy waste and slashing carbon emissions. Going further, micro-generation can be enhanced by a Feed-in Tariff (FIT). This is simply rewarding homeowners for producing their own solar, wind or hydroelectricity and the results are transformative. Germany's FIT has resulted in 12 per cent of their energy being renewable and the industry has provided a quarter of a million jobs. The UK has lagged behind for long enough.

So once the energy has reached our homes, there are yet more problems in efficiency. As ever, there is a practical remedy. The 25 million homes in the UK account for almost a quarter of Britain's greenhouse gas emissions. A huge number of these lack insulation and effective window glazing. Retrofitting every house in the UK could save £12 billion a year, so why isn't it being done? The answer is, primarily, because it requires a lot of money in the short term. Given that it's a low risk investment (cavity wall insulation has a payback time of three years and then brings considerable savings), why not utilise the funds in the Green Investment Bank or, dare I say it, attract investment from the private sector? If we combine to this our policy of installing a smart meter in every home by 2020, we can make further substantial reductions in energy costs and carbon emissions. Substantial, but not sufficient. The only path to sufficient reductions is to end our reliance on fossil fuels.

Ask what our greatest natural asset is and it's unlikely that the response would be our seas – indeed they are. The last Labour Government predicted that by 2025, nearly 25 per cent of our energy could be produced from offshore wind and 12.5 per cent from tidal. Discovering North Sea oil bankrolled Margaret Thatcher's early years and brought over 300 international companies to Aberdeen. It would have defied sense for her to ignore North Sea oil but that's the equivalent of what we're doing today. Although it is easy for private companies to build the turbines and wave power generators, they can't do that without a grid. Labour should commit to a policy of investing in the seabed cables that will provide the opportunity for offshore wind and tidal power to flourish. It already exists in Cornwall; we simply need it replicated across our remaining 7,760 miles of coastline. Whilst this makes strides, it still won't fully meet our energy needs. Some environmentalists make the case for Carbon Capture Storage (removing carbon dioxide from coal emissions) but the technology is decades away and thus commercially unviable. We already have a carbon-free alternative – nuclear. Although there is ample reason to loathe the nuclear industry, avoiding climate change dictates that there is a need to compromise. Nuclear provides the least worst option by being a reliable, tested and carbon free energy supply. We must also understand that disasters like Chernobyl and Fukushima don't apply to us – we maintain our nuclear plants unlike Soviet Ukraine and are tectonic opposites of Japan. Nuclear energy is safer than policymakers and greens make out and, however reluctantly, we have to pursue it.

All these solutions – micro-generation, retrofitting and renewables – they're not a product of idealism and naivety. They all exist and work successfully today and Labour must learn from them and replicate them. Ignoring the minority that complain about blotted landscapes and taking the compelling argument to the electorate that this will leave us less vulnerable to far off geopolitics and save money on our energy bills can bring us, not only electoral gains, but most importantly the green economy that, at the moment, is just rhetoric.

Ecology

Food, water and air – we all need them so it's remarkable they aren't higher on our political agenda, particularly when they're under the threats they currently are. Despite soaring food prices and frequent food riots across the world, the dominant thinking in the UK is that we can import food from abroad and therefore not worry about it. Not only does this mean a much higher cost in carbon but it has brought UK farming near to extinction and left farmers to the mercy of the market. In the past few years, we have lost up to 1,000 farms a week. If hospitals, schools, prisons and similar services were required to provide, where possible, locally sourced food, it would bring a desperately needed boost to the farming industry as well as to the nation's health. Throughout the rest of Europe, the Common Agricultural Policy competes unfairly with the poorest farmers and places a stranglehold on them due to unnecessarily raising food prices. If we instead reform CAP to reward farmers who use their land sustainably, as the market doesn't currently do, we will begin to see a recovering farming industry and a more diverse, available food supply that we don't have to import.

In greater decline than our farms are the world's fish stocks. In 1968, the registered catch in Newfoundland was 800,000 tonnes each year. By 1994, it was 1,700 tonnes. The Canadian government was forced to issue a two-year moratorium and over 40,000 people lost their livelihoods. The Newfoundland disaster occurred because of the rampant desire for profit, manifested in 'draggers', immense ships that dredged the ocean floors destroying every variety of fish and entire ecosystems. These ships were not unique to Newfoundland; they're still used today and are largely the reason why 80 per cent of the world's fish stocks are in a similar state of exploitation and depletion. The other tools that threaten the existence of our fish stocks are the sixty-mile-wide nets carrying 10 billion baited hooks globally that similarly kill everything in their paths including inedible fish and endangered species. The simple solution is to ban these tools outright. They cannot exist alongside sustainable fishing. Despite the pessimism of the current situation, we can find hope in two facts. First, the oceans' ability to recover is remarkable so when the pressure on them is eased, fish populations soar. Secondly, most fish populations are around coasts so the issue is a sovereign, not a national one which makes solving this easier. If we designate areas around our coasts as Marine Protected Areas, we will begin to see fish stocks recover. We should lobby other governments to do the same.

Whilst we've depleted our fish stocks, we've destroyed nearly half of the world's rainforests. The first Labour leader to speak out against rainforest destruction was Keir Hardie and this is a tradition we need to continue. Their vital services go entirely unvalued. They regulate rainfall and fresh water globally, store 50 per cent more carbon than the atmosphere and are home to 50 per cent of the world's species. The case for protecting them is indisputable but nearly every government is reluctant to do so. One immediate policy Labour should adopt is to ban the trade in illegal timber and ensure the public sector, which accounts for 40 per cent of timber purchases in the UK, sources all its timber sustainably. The rest must be solved internationally. This requires a constructive, pro-active voice in the EU and UN, which is why Labour is best suited to lobbying for higher standards and tighter restrictions in rainforest use. This is an area in which we can't remain inactive.

We're exhausting the very systems we depend on. In the face of population growth and our increasing hunger for resources, the Earth cannot meet these demands. Oil is running out. Energy bills are rising and people already suffer from the effects of climate change. This has been said time and time again to the point where it goes in one ear and out the other. With this in mind, my last suggestion for Labour is how to sell these policies to the electorate.

That these policies need to be implemented to avoid environmental catastrophe is true, but at the moment this won't persuade enough people to vote for them. Labour needs to create its own message on climate change because the scare tactics of rising temperatures and sea levels, although real, haven't worked. Our environmentalism is protecting the poorest from fuel poverty, protecting the most vulnerable from increased droughts and food shortages and increasing the living standards of all people irrespective of class. The People's Party needs to discover that without this, we'll never bring about social justice. And if we help save the planet along the way, that's just a bonus.

Graham Stringer MP

Transport Policy for the Twenty-First Century

Graham served as a Councillor for 16 years, including serving as Leader of Manchester City Council. He was active in promoting Manchester's bid to host the 2002 Commonwealth Games, which has enabled him to promote Manchester and the North West on an international stage. He was a member of the Manchester Airport Board, and Chair of Manchester Airport. He was elected to Parliament in 1997, and was appointed as Parliamentary Secretary for the Cabinet Office in 1999; he has served as a Government Whip, and currently sits on the Science and Technology Committee and the Transport Committee.

Tony Blair famously stated that Labour's top three priorities in government were Education, Education and Education. The corollary was left unstated that other mainstream public services were not the priority. In 2001 health moved into top position with education when the Labour Prime Minister proclaimed that health spending would increase to the European average, this led to a trebling of expenditure in cash terms on health.

Transport therefore was never really the focus of attention of the last Labour Government and when expenditure did increase it was often in response to a crisis and not the conclusion of a thought through transport or economic policy.

The railway system for instance, received a huge increase in public subsidy after major train crashes had shown that under Network Rail our railways were simply not safe. They went from receiving about £1 billion a year, which was expected to diminish to zero, to an annual subsidy of £4-5 billion a year.

The railways have achieved the financially extraordinary feat of having record numbers of passengers paying higher fares and receiving more public subsidy; only a Tory privatisation scheme could have produced such a perverse result.

Similarly buses, outside London, had a fivefold increase in subsidy but in a deregulated system this also had many perverse consequences. In rural areas large numbers of services disappeared altogether, while in urban areas networks shrank and fares increased as the bus operator developed business plans that were directed at maximising public subsidy, not providing a service for passengers. Passengers fled the system in their millions while the profits of bus companies rose.

Everything was of course very different in London's regulated system where Labour Mayor Ken Livingstone increased the subsidy to buses and expanded both the daytime and night time networks; passengers returned to one of the best bus systems in the world.

The funding of buses and trains was not the only area where transport spending priorities and their results were curious to say the least. In every major funding block, London gets more subsidy per head of population than the rest of the country. This is unwelcome but easily explained by higher costs of land and wages in London. What no Labour minister was able to explain was why it was only in transport that the gap widened. So as Labour increased the funding in health and education, the ratio of per capita expenditure between London and the English regions remained the same. Not so in transport, between 2000 and 2005 the ratio between London and the English regions went from 2 to 1 to 3 to 1, this imbalance is still increasing.

This was not a political decision but the consequence of the methodology used by the Department of Transport to justify investment in transport infrastructure. The Department used congestion as the main justification, for investment which results in most of the transport money going to London.

Transport nearly always stimulates economic activity and such creation. The investment therefore does not help the congestion and overcrowding but creates more imbalance between London and the English regions. It is in effect a subsidy for congestion! The same investment in Newcastle or Manchester say would create jobs and also decrease the congestion in London.

I have summarised very generally some of the big spending changes on transport during the period of the last Labour Government. I don't think any Labour politician in 1997 would have chosen to take these decisions with their perverse consequences. We need to learn the lessons from the deprivatisation of transport and take a much more strategic approach during the next Labour Government, seeing transport as not just an end itself but a vital part of an economic strategy to support growth, reverse regional imbalances and to help the socially excluded and marginalised.

Interestingly, this was the objection to John Prescott's White Paper planning transport for the next ten years at the start of the last Labour Government. He had not only moved the Department of Transport into a new department with environmental, regional and economic responsibilities, he saw transport policy as the crucial area in order to reduce pollution, help the socially excluded and improve the regional economies.

John failed and his department was broken up but the White Paper continued many of the priorities that should be key for the next Labour Government. One of the fundamentals that was never tackled was the fact that motoring has been getting cheaper in real terms and public transport more expensive. Unless that issue is tackled any policy that prioritises public transport is going to fail. People will vote with their wallets.

To take just one example the White Paper envisaged 20 new tram systems in the country. They didn't happen because the large amounts of money spent on transport were wasted, not because they were unaffordable. If Railtrack had not been such a disaster, the extra money put into the railways would easily have paid for 20 new tram systems.

I will look at four areas of transport policy where Labour could make a huge difference and get it right next time.

Buses

More than two thirds of public transport journeys are taken on buses. The figure is higher for many cities. For the poorest communities buses provide their only access to jobs, leisure and healthcare.

The number of people using buses has been in long-term decline since the early 1950s. This unwelcomed trend has been driven by the increase in costs of travel by public transport and the decrease in cost of car travel, in real terms. This long term change in travel patterns was exacerbated in 1985 when the then Conservative Government deregulated buses everywhere in the United Kingdom except London and Northern Ireland. Having two different systems operating within our country gives us the opportunity to compare the relative merits of both systems. A brief description of the regulated and deregulated system I think would be helpful.

In a regulated system, the local transport authority issues licenses to private bus companies to run bus services. The awarding of these licenses follows a tendering process during which the bus companies can compete with each other to run given networks to specified schedules and fares. This gives control to the councillors on the transport authority of the networks, fares and schedules. Depending on the nature of the network schedules and fares the bus company may have to pay cash for the contract or receive a grant, but once the tender is agreed there is a stable bus service provided for the public.

In a deregulated system elected councillors have no role. Bus companies inform the transport authority which services they are going to run and on which routes. They can change this notification at very short notice and they retain control of fares. If, as is often the case, this leads to an inadequate network with some communities not receiving any bus services at all or only at peak times, the transport authority can put out tenders on a route by route basis.

To summarise – the deregulated system has competition on the road and the regulated system has competition at the tendering stage. There is a large amount of evidence that in a deregulated system bus companies enter into cartels in order not to compete and also force up the cost when individual rates are put out for tender. There is no doubt that the regulated system offers a more stable and less expensive system and is better for passengers and the environment.

After 1985 the London system remained essentially unchanged both in subsidies and routes and there was no drop off in passengers. Fares remained stable, by comparison, in Greater Manchester in the 20 years after deregulation, passenger journeys declined by 147 million from 355 million per annum to 258 million per annum. In the deregulated system, competition bus companies focused on the heavily used radial roads and passengers were abandoned in more remote locations. This was very inefficient, it has been established that on the removed networks there were 10% more buses on the roads than in the regulated system carrying less passengers and causing congestion. Deregulated service was also extremely expensive, each bus leaving a depot had already received subsidies of more than half its running cost.

It was not surprising therefore, the profitability of this system at the expense of the travelling public enabled the large bus companies to transform themselves into large multinational companies. It cannot have been the objective of the Labour Government to turn the directors of these companies into multi-millionaires while passengers were left stranded and led to pay higher fares. The system killed off any prospect of having an integrated transport system because through ticketing between the different bus companies was outlawed by the competition authorities. It was one of Labour's great embarrassments not to reregulate the buses during its 13 years in office although towards the end of its time in power it passed the 2008 Transport Act which provided a pathway back to regulation for Transport Authorities, albeit in a very complicated and burdensome way.

The next Labour Government should make it a priority to improve on this regulation and make re- regulation easier. Bus companies presently receive a subsidy to the fuel they use called the Bus Service Operation Grant (BSOG). This money should be passed over to the Transport Authority so it can be used for bus operators to invest in less polluting buses with better disabled access and to attract them back into a regulated system.

It is primarily Labour's voters who use buses, there are many parts of our great urban conurbations where more than half the households do not have access to a private car.

Free travel for the over 60s is enormously popular and has been a great success. We must make sure that there are buses available for people with bus passes as well as everybody else by making re-regulation a top priority.

Light Rail and Trams
While buses have been shedding passengers, trams have been attracting more and new passengers. Reasons for this are complex, but reliability and fashion seem to be a huge factor. Middle aged business men will happily leave their BMW at home

and hop on a tram while they wouldn't be seen dead on a bus.

Trams have not received the investment they require because of the huge amount of money sucked into heavy rail following the disaster of Railtrack. The second reason why trams have been neglected is that they are not on a level playing field with buses. The Department of Transport unfairly compares investment in trams and light rail with revenue subsidy for buses. The initial investment in trams is very high, but academic studies have shown that over a 20 year period it is better value for money (or at least the same) as the continuing revenue subsidy for buses. The investment in light rail is also a long term commitment to public transport; buses can receive their funding and then be moved to another route or city; once the investment in trams is made it is there for a generation. An incoming Labour Government should recommit to the tram systems that John Prescott originally committed to whilst he served at the Department for Transport.

Trains

When the last Labour government came into office, it rejected calls to renationalise the railways. Its argument was simple, if you paid private companies £x billion for the railways, you ended up with the same rail infrastructure but the £x billion could not be invested in health, education or transport, as it would be in the bank balances of the private concerns that owned the railways. This was a good argument but was confounded by experience. The demise of Railtrack, the creation of Network Rail and franchising system has left us with one of the most costly railways in the world. To take one example, access charges for freight are twice the industry norm and Network Rail which is a quasi public body, has overhead costs more than four times British Rail's and carries more than £20 billion of debt on its balance sheet. Train operating companies with long and short franchises have failed, investment always tails off at the end of the franchise period and the cost to the franchising companies has stopped them spending money.

The overall financial structure of the franchises has crazy implications for public investments. When the Government invested £7.5 billion upgrading the West Coast Line, they also compensated Virgin the franchise holder for the disruption i.e. the Government paid twice to improve Virgin's profitability. An incoming Labour Government should restore Network Rail back to the public sector so that it is democratically accountable. Franchises should be phased out so that we end up with a publically owned railway system. Privatisation has been tried and failed.

High Speed Rail
The case for High Speed Rail is overwhelmingly an economic case, to help restore the regional economic imbalance between the English regions and London and the South East. Labour should insist that the hybrid Bill, soon to be before Parliament, should not stop at Birmingham but should give alignments to Manchester and Leeds and determine the location of stations in Manchester and Leeds. It is also vital that the northern rail system is electrified, its capacity increased along the lines envisaged in the Northern Hub proposals. High Speed 2 will only be economically viable if it goes to Manchester and Leeds and preferably also to Glasgow and Edinburgh. We should give a long term commitment to this vital project.

Aviation
"Without the ability to efficiently transport business, leisure travellers and time sensitive cargo, both domestic and international business would grind to a halt – the leading economic sectors- financial and business services, tourism, pharmaceuticals, media and communications, higher education and research and development- all rely on frequent air travel to

many destinations – having too few flights to handle demand will prevent millions from flying and cost the country and its regions thousands of jobs and billions of pounds". This is a modified quote from a report on the future of New York's aviation business, but applies perfectly to the United Kingdom. The decision by the Coalition Government not to build a third runway at Heathrow has meant that this country's main airport now serves fewer destinations than Frankfurt, Munich, Madrid, Paris and Amsterdam. This means that we are less well connected to the growing BRIC economies than all our main competitors.

There is no realistic alternative but to retain our commitment to a third runway at Heathrow. The restriction of access to London and the South East actually increases the air pollution as passengers from the United Kingdom have to use other hubs and therefore have to take off and land twice in order to get to their destination. Lack of access to Heathrow is also bad for businesses in the rest of the United Kingdom. The regional airports and the country have also been hit by Air Passenger Duty which should be abolished when the European Emissions Trading Scheme is introduced next year. Air Passenger Duty is driving tourists from Asia and the Americas into other European countries where they do not have a passenger tax. Aviation is nearly 2% of our gross domestic product but it is much more important than this, because without links to emerging economies, the United Kingdom's trade will be damaged.

Roads

The United Kingdom has the lowest motorway density of any of our major European competitors. A major pinch point in the system should be widened like the M6 north of Birmingham and the system should be expanded to major economic centres that are not served by motorways, like Bootle Docks.

It is quite clear that the electorate will not stand for congestion charging and therefore a simple solution that satisfies the principle of the polluter pays, would be to reduce road tax to say £25 and raise the rest of the lost tax by raising fuel duty.

Labour needs to place greater importance on transport policy. If we are to have transport fit for the future then we must be willing to consider making the investment in our transport infrastructure that is necessary to bring it into the 21st Century.

Dr Nick Palmer

Animal welfare:
The Neglected Swing Issue

*Nick Palmer was Labour MP for Broxtowe from 1997 to 2010.
He is currently Director of Policy at the BUAV, one of Britain's
leading animal protection campaigns*

One of the key elements of the pre-1997 landslide was that Labour didn't simply rely on the "18 wasted years" line and the mess that the Tories had made of the economy. We offered fresh alternative policies in an extraordinarily wide range of areas, giving voters the sense that there was something interesting to support rather than merely something to reject.

One of the highlights was the "New Life for Animals" mini-manifesto, with pledges ranging from a ban on fur farming to a vote on fox-hunting, from improved farm animal conditions to a full review of animal experiment legislation. As a PPC in that year, I found that the A3 leaflet presenting this was shifting votes to us from people without the slightest Labour leanings in any other respects. It's one of those issues which, for those who care about it, override party allegiance.

Labour went on to implement the fur farm ban and make at least some improvements in farm animal welfare. The fox-hunting ban eventually staggered over the line despite Tony's all too evident lack of enthusiasm, and the Animal Welfare Act was the first umbrella legislation for nearly a century, giving the potential for major improvements. However, in subsequent elections we said less and less about animal welfare, and the 2010 manifesto was completely silent on the subject. This reflected a gradual narrowing of our agenda: Labour was overwhelmingly about saving the economy and protecting public services, and very little else.

In the face of the global crisis and worn down by 13 years in power, it's not too hard to understand how that happened. However, we need to expand our horizons again. If we purely pitch our argument on economic competence, we are putting our fate in the hands of the global economy. If that recovers, Britain will eventually recover too, and we shouldn't put all our eggs in the 'reject Tory disaster' basket. Labour needs to offer positive hope as well; for the environment, for education, for health – and, yes, for animal welfare.

Is there much to do on animal welfare? There is indeed. Britain likes to think of itself as animal-friendly, but the reality is very mixed. Here are a few suggestions:

1. Get serious about reducing animal experiments. They fell under the Tories up to 1997 and rose under Labour. We cannot afford to leave the issue of exploitation of animals to the right of the political spectrum. That doesn't mean that experiments suddenly disappear overnight, but that Labour pledges a steady reduction – for instance, through a tax on project licences for animal experiments balanced by a subsidy for non-animal research, or a ban on the deliberate inflicting of psychological suffering in order to study its effects. The polls are overwhelmingly in favour of ending non-medical animal experiments (which make up the majority), we should at least be committed to reversing the rising trend.

2. Get serious about reducing intensive farming. This and animal experiments are the two areas involving the most animals, and the way that free-range eggs have almost driven battery eggs off the shelves is testimony to the clear consumer preference for better treatment. This is an area where a Pro-European party can show just how effective the EU can be: better standards for farm animals required across the gigantic EU market will lead through to become a global requirement as well, simply because farmers want to be able to sell to the EU.

3. Make the hunting ban work. We've ended up with a very British fudge: hunting with hounds is sort of illegal, and it's partially enforced, making life awkward for hunts without really stopping them. Plenty of people who don't really care about the issue don't like to see the law blatantly flouted.

4. Ban performing animals in circuses. This should be a no-brainer – there are now very few, and most of the public has long since stopped enjoying the spectacle of wild animals forced into artificial performances in the ring. It doesn't even need primary legislation – we can do it under the Animal Welfare Act.

5. End the badger cull. This anti-scientific policy was rightly rejected by the last government. Briefly, if you exterminate badgers in an area, you speed up the arrival of badgers from neighbouring areas as they fill the vacuum, thereby accelerating the circulation of infection. Introduced on a "something must be done" basis to appease the National Farmers' Union, the policy will be ripe for termination by the time of the next election.

The vested interests who dominate factory farming and animal experiments always suggest that we should be focusing on human suffering – why worry about a pig when you could worry about a child? But why should we accept this false choice? Amoebas are probably only able to consider one thought at a time: those of us with more than one cell should be able to work to reduce cruelty and exploitation towards both humans and animals.

Isn't that, ultimately, what brought most of us into the Labour Party?

End Notes

1   eg the *Independent* recently stated "Suburbs and small towns can appear the very essence of parochialism, mediocrity and conformity" (29/12/10)

2   Marshall, John. (2009). Membership of UK political parties. House of Commons Library (SN/SG/5125)

3   Watt, Peter. We don't see it, but our arrogance stops us from listening. The Labour Uncut Blog. December 2, 2010. http://labour-uncut.co.uk/2010/12/02/6080/

4   Fox, Dr Ruth. (2010). What's trust got to do with it? (pp. 5 – 9). Hansard Society, Political Studies Association and Centre for Citizenship, Globalization and Governance. ISBN – 978 0900432 69 9

5   Akehurst, Luke. Building the Party. luke's blog. November 16, 2010. http://lukeakehurst.blogspot.com/search?q=organisation

6   Paul Swinney, Kieran Larkin, Chris Webber, *Firm Intentions: Cities, Private Sector Jobs & The Coalition,* (Centre for Cities, 2010)

7   Ed Cox, *Five Foundations of Real Localism,* (IPPR, November 2010)

8   Kieran Larkin, *Regional Development Agencies: the Facts,* (Centre for Cities, 2009)

9   *The Times,* 8 December 2010

10 Citied in Paul Richards, *Labour's Revival, The Modernisers Manifesto,* (2010)

[11] Miles, Alice, "The truth is that Lansley's NHS plan doesn't go far enough", in New Statesman, 16 May 2011, p 23

[12] Williams, Rowan, "The government needs to know how afraid people are", in New Statesman, 13 June 2011, p 4

[13] Anthony Parker Mar 22, 2011, Harnessing the new generation, http://www.labourlist.org/harnessing-the-new-generation

[14] Hasan, Mehdi, "Enough of these hazy, vacuous and contradictory attacks on Miliband", in New Statesman, 30 May 2011, p 12.

[15] Miliband, Ed, preface, in "The Labour tradition and the politics of paradox", The Oxford London seminars 2010-2011, eds Maurice Glasman, Jonathan Rutherford, Marc Stears and Stuart White, p 8

[16] Landrum, David, series forward, in Bickley, P, "Building Jerusalem? Christianity and the Labour Party", Bible Society, Swindon, 2010, p 1

[17] Reeves, Richard, (2009), What next for Labour? Ideas for the progressive left, http://www.demos.co.uk/files/What_next_for_ Labour_.pdf?1244746884 p 7

[18] Marquand, David, (2009), "Wait for the next St Paul", in What next for Labour? Ideas for the progressive left, http://www.demos.co.uk/ files/What_next_for_Labour_.pdf?1244746884 p 87

[19] "Blair's Community: Communitarian Thought and New Labour Community" in Development Journal (2008) 43(2): 259-261 http://cdj.oxfordjournals.org/content/43/2/259.extract

[20] Merrett, Kieron http://kieronam.net/?p=107 January 12, 2011

[21] Rutherford, Jonathan & Shah Hetan, in "The Good Society", Compass programme for Renewal, Lawrence and Wishart Ltd, 2006

[22] Chaplin, Jonathan (2011) "Why a "Just Society" must also be a "Big Society", http://www.cardus.ca/policy/article/2812/

[23] Glasman, Maurce, ' Labour as a radical tradition' in "The Labour tradition and the politics of paradox", The Oxford London seminars 2010-2011, eds Maurice Glasman, Jonathan Rutherford, Marc Stears and Stuart White, p 27

[24] Bickley, Paul, "Building Jerusalem? Christianity and the Labour Party", Bible Society, Swindon, 2010, p 7

[25] Green, James (2011) http://www.labourlist.org/we-dont-do-god-but-should-we

[26] Cruddas, Jon (2011) http://www.thecsm.org.uk/Articles/160983/Christian_Socialist_Movement/Articles/The_Common_Good/Issue_200_Feeling/Interview_with_Jon.aspx

[27] Hasan, Mehdi (2010) http://www.newstatesman.com/religion/2010/12/jesus-god-tax-christ-health

[28] Peterson, Eugene, "The Message The Old Testament Prophets" Navpress, Colorado, Navpress, 2000, p 136

[29] Lord Leitch, 'Prosperity for all in the global economy – world class skills'

http://www.official-documents.gov.uk/document/other/
0118404792/0118404792.pdf

30 Lord Sainsbury, 'The race to the top'
http://www.rsc.org/images/sainsbury_review051007_tcm18-
103116.pdf

31 HM Government, 'Opening Doors, Breaking Barriers: A Strategy
for Social Mobility' http://download.cabinetoffice.gov.uk/social-
mobility/opening-doors-breaking-barriers.pdf

32 Commonwealth Fund: How Health Insurance Design Affects
Access to care and Costs, by Income, in eleven countries –
November 18, 2010

33 British Social Attitudes 27th Report

34 Parliamentary and Health Service Ombudsman: Care and
Compassion? February 2011

35 The NHS Plan: a plan for investment, a plan for reform – July
2000, Department of Health

Additional Bibliography:

Dr Rupa Huq:

- Diamond, P. and Radice, G. (2010) "Southern Discomfort Again". London: Policy Network at **www.policynetwork.net/publications_download.a spx?ID=7134**
- Lott, T. (2009) "Why uncertainty is good for you," in *Sunday Times* 24/5/09 at **http://women.timesonline.co.uk/tol/life_and_styl e/women/the_way_we_live/article6320285.ece**
- McGhee, D. (2010) *Security, Citizenship & Human Rights: Shared Values in Uncertain Times*. Basingstoke: Palgrave.
- RCUK (2010) http://www.globaluncertainties.org.uk/
- Reeves, R. (2007) '*Middle England*: *they're nicer* than you think', New Statesman 25/10/07 at http://www.newstatesman.com/politics/2007/10/middle-england-class-social

Index